OUTSTANDING
STORIES
by General
Authorities

OUTSTANDING STORIES by General Authorities

Volume 2

Compiled by LEON R. HARTSHORN

Published by
DESERET BOOK COMPANY
Salt Lake City, Utah
1971

Library of Congress Catalog Card No. 73-136241
ISBN No. 87747-467-2

LITHOGRAPHED BY

DESERET NEWS PRESS

IN THE UNITED STATES OF AMERICA

Table of Contents

Page

Elder Joseph Anderson

Picture - x
Biographical Sketch - 1
"Give Heber $10,000" - 3
"A True Servant of God" - 5
"Brother Grant It's My Turn Next" - - - - - - - - - - - - - - - 7

Elder Marvin J. Ashton

Picture - 10
Biographical Sketch - 11
"I'll Never Get in Anyone's Way" - - - - - - - - - - - - - - - - 13
"He Is An Old Grouch Today" - - - - - - - - - - - - - - - - - - 14
"A Silver Dollar in My Hand" - - - - - - - - - - - - - - - - - - 15
"He's For Sale Pretty Cheap" - - - - - - - - - - - - - - - - - - 16

Elder Ezra Taft Benson

Picture - 18
Biographical Sketch - 19
"How Old Are You?" - 23
"Well, What You Want Is A Returned Mormon Missionary" - - 24
"More Loyal Support for One Another" - - - - - - - - - - - - - 26
"A Day Which I Shall Never Forget" - - - - - - - - - - - - - - - 27
"Mr. Governor, Would You Believe Such a Thing Could
    Happen?" - 28
"Separation For A Period of Two Years" - - - - - - - - - - - - - 29
"That Was President Smith" - 30
"They Just Stood There and Visited and Visited" - - - - - - - - 31
"Twenty-Two People Were Living in One Room" - - - - - - - - 33
"From Somewhere They Had Obtained An Old Radio" - - - - - - 34
"Many of These Saints Dressed in Rags" - - - - - - - - - - - - - 36

Bishop Victor L. Brown

Picture - 40
Biographical Sketch - 41
"What Do You Mean, Milk?" - - - - - - - - - - - - - - - - - - - 43
"It's Serving Our Fellowmen" - - - - - - - - - - - - - - - - - - - 45
"Sione Rose From His Knees" - - - - - - - - - - - - - - - - - - - 46
"He Was Entranced with the Story of the Gospel" - - - - - - - - 48
"Let's Let Him Make That Decision" - - - - - - - - - - - - - - - 49

Elder Matthew Cowley

Page

Picture - 54
Biographical Sketch - 55
  "Oneness of Direction" - 59
  "We Are Fasting and Praying" - - - - - - - - - - - - - - - - - - 60
  "I'm Ready Now to Bless Your Boy" - - - - - - - - - - - - - - 61
  "What On Earth Will I Do?" - - - - - - - - - - - - - - - - - - 62
  "Secretary of the Relief Society" - - - - - - - - - - - - - - - - 63
  "He Was An Unusual Boy" - - - - - - - - - - - - - - - - - - - 64
  "Fix Me Up, I Want To Go Home" - - - - - - - - - - - - - - - 66
  "Just as Miraculous As Raising the Dead" - - - - - - - - - - - 67
  "The Doctor Isn't Home" - 68
  "I Can't Say That About My Church" - - - - - - - - - - - - - 69
  "They Fed the Lovely Parents" - - - - - - - - - - - - - - - - - 70
  "The Mortgage Is Paid Off" - - - - - - - - - - - - - - - - - - 71
  "You Do Not Owe That Much Tithing" - - - - - - - - - - - - 72
  "Then I Am Safe for Another Week" - - - - - - - - - - - - - - 73
  "I Walked Fearlessly" - 74
  "See What You Have Done For Me" - - - - - - - - - - - - - - 75
  "That One Day Was Spent in the Temple" - - - - - - - - - - - 76
  "She's Physically Well from Head to Foot" - - - - - - - - - - - 77
  "I Received A Message" - 78
  "Medical Science Had Laid the Burden Down" - - - - - - - - - 80
  "Send for the Elders" - 80
  "Give Him His Vision" - 81

President Loren C. Dunn

Picture - 84
Biographical Sketch - 85
  "When We Recognize the Priesthood" - - - - - - - - - - - - - 87
  "Who Is Going to Care?" - 88
  "My Father Never Gave Up On Me" - - - - - - - - - - - - - - 90
  "One Electrifying Moment" - - - - - - - - - - - - - - - - - - - 91
  "To Me, This Is the Generation Gap" - - - - - - - - - - - - - 92
  "Splinters of Glass" - 93
  "I Had Made the Wrong Decision" - - - - - - - - - - - - - - 94
  "We Will be Spiritually Dead" - - - - - - - - - - - - - - - - - 95
  "Clinging to A Fence" - 96

President Paul H. Dunn

Picture - 98
Biographical Sketch - 99
  "His Name Was Lou Gehrig" - - - - - - - - - - - - - - - - - - 101
  "A Standing Ovation" - 105
  "Now If You Want an Interview, Listen" - - - - - - - - - - - - 107
  "I Was a New Board Member" - - - - - - - - - - - - - - - - - 108
  "Where Do You Sign Up?" - - - - - - - - - - - - - - - - - - - 110
  "Two Can Play This Game" - - - - - - - - - - - - - - - - - - - 113
  "A Tiny Speck of Dirt" - 114
  "Let's See If You Really Mean That" - - - - - - - - - - - - - - 115
  "Not Ashamed to Be Identified" - - - - - - - - - - - - - - - - 116
  "Paul Dunn, Come Up Here" - - - - - - - - - - - - - - - - - - 117

	Page
"I'll Race You to the Parking Lot"	119
"Can You Qualify?"	120
"The New Testament Came Very Forcefully to My Mind"	122
"Elder, It Looks Like You've Been Through a Famine"	124
"There Is Nothing I Don't Know"	125
"Happiness Is Being Able to Walk"	127
"Builder of Men"	129
"Do You Have An American Flag?"	130

Elder Alvin R. Dyer

Picture	132
Biographical Sketch	133
"Father Wants You To Come Back"	137
"Dr. Novinski"	138
"They Had No Permit"	141

Elder Spencer W. Kimball

Picture	144
Biographical Sketch	145
"That First Tithing Receipt"	149
"Still Smiling, In Her Wheel Chair"	150
"Carry A Message to Garcia"	151
"The Breaking of Day Has Found Me on My Knees"	153
"You Will See Him Someday as a Great Leader"	155
"The Story of Lazarus"	156
"Guests of the Lord"	158

Elder Mark E. Petersen

Picture	162
Biographical Sketch	163
"I Was Blind"	165
"A Friend of Mine Whom I Shall Call Bill"	166
"Dare to Be a Mormon"	172
"Who Is Responsible?"	173
"On My Honor"	175

President Hartman Rector, Jr.

Picture	178
Biographical Sketch	179
"Radio Tubes"	181
"Your Decisions Will *Make You*"	183
"Close Enough to the Angels"	186
"My Spirit Is Nine Feet Tall"	188
"It Is What's Inside That Really Counts"	190
"He Really Passed the Test"	191
"You Do It If You Are Going to Be Honest"	192
"A Tower of Strength"	194
"He Reached for the Cigarette"	195

Bishop Robert L. Simpson

Page

Picture - 198
Biographical Sketch - 199
    "Just a Few Pennies a Day" - - - - - - - - - - - - - - - - - - - 201
    "Charting a Course" - 202
    "This Young Lady Was Loyal" - - - - - - - - - - - - - - - - - - 204
    "Right into My Hands" - 206
    "You Are Going to Jump Up and Down" - - - - - - - - - - - - 207
    "It Sounded True, It Sounded Real" - - - - - - - - - - - - - - 209
    "The Game of Life" - 210
    "Were You On Noah's Ark?" - - - - - - - - - - - - - - - - - - - 211
    "Be a Good Receiver" - 211
    "Welfare Work in Action" - 215
    "Good Samaritan" - 216
    "But Daddy, I Wasn't Talking to You" - - - - - - - - - - - - - 219

Patriarch Eldred G. Smith

Picture - 220
Biographical Sketch - 221
    "What a Patriarchal Blessing Can Do" - - - - - - - - - - - - - 223
    "I Met the Challenge" - 225
    "I Am Healed, I Am Well" - 226
    "Why Should We Question the Resurrection?" - - - - - - - - - 227
    "The Only Ones Sitting in the Audience" - - - - - - - - - - - 230
    "This Is Priesthood Order" - - - - - - - - - - - - - - - - - - - 232
    "He Had Quit Several Times" - - - - - - - - - - - - - - - - - - 234
    "How Did You Know?" - 236
    "Bishop, I See What You Came Here to Tell Me" - - - - - - - 237

Bishop John H. Vandenberg

Picture - 238
Biographical Sketch - 239
    "Following Counsel" - 241
    "Thanks for the Lesson" - 242
    "The True Fiber" - 244
    "The Most Wonderful Thing in the World" - - - - - - - - - - - 246
    "Now You Can Get Further Behind" - - - - - - - - - - - - - - 247
    "My Father Works There" - - - - - - - - - - - - - - - - - - - 249
    "Home Plate Doesn't Move" - - - - - - - - - - - - - - - - - - 249
    "I Guess You'll Have to Walk" - - - - - - - - - - - - - - - - - 250
    "My Dearest Father Bishopric" - - - - - - - - - - - - - - - - 251
    "We Now Have Two Healthy Lambs" - - - - - - - - - - - - - 252

Biographical Sketch

Elder Joseph Anderson, named an Assistant to the Council of The Twelve of The Church of Jesus Christ of Latter-day Saints, April 6, 1970, had been secretary to the First Presidency of the Church since 1923.

Elder Anderson continues with his secretarial assignments, serving as clerk of the general conferences of the Church twice each year, recording conference speeches and proceedings and keeping minutes and attending meetings of the First Presidency and the Council of Twelve.

Elder Anderson was born in Salt Lake City, Utah, on November 20, 1889. He was graduated from Weber Academy, now Weber State College, at the age of 15.

He was a missionary for the Church in Switzerland and Germany from 1911 to 1914. After a brief business career in Salt Lake City, he became secretary to late Church President Heber J. Grant. Since then he has traveled throughout the world with the presidents of the Church on their various assignments.

For twenty-five years, Elder Anderson was a member of the Bonneville Stake High Council in Salt Lake City. Prior to that he was a member of the bishopric of the Thirty-Third Ward and Sunday School superintendent.

1

For many years he has been director, member of the executive committee, and secretary-treasurer of the Deseret Book Company in Salt Lake City.

He married Norma Peterson in the Salt Lake Temple on Nov. 11, 1915. They have a son and two daughters.

JOSEPH ANDERSON

"Give Heber $10,000"

There is another story I would like to tell you that President Grant often told. Whenever the Church needed someone to collect funds for some important purpose, they called on Brother Grant. At the time, of course, he was an apostle. And he was a great financier and a wonderful man for contributing to funds and for collecting funds. On one occasion, it so happened that one of the banks in Salt Lake was in trouble, and it looked like it might fail. Some of the Brethren were interested in the bank as directors, and if it had failed, it would have been quite an embarrassment to them. And the President of the Church called on Brother Grant to go out and collect funds that they might put into the bank to save it from disaster.

Now some people questioned the wisdom of that, but at any rate Brother Grant went forward on his mission. And one of the places he visited was Provo where he called on Jesse Knight and Reed Smoot. He asked Reed Smoot for $2,000, and he asked Jesse for $5,000. They were both men of means, Brother Knight particularly, as some of you well know.

Jesse wasn't altogether sold on the idea. He said, "No, I

don't think that an apostle of the Lord ought to be going out gathering funds for that purpose. I don't think that that's a worthy cause to go out and make collections for."

And Brother Smoot said, "I'll give you $1,000, but I won't give you $2,000."

Brother Grant said, "Brother Smoot, you have offered $1,000. I'll not take it, but you go home tonight and get down on your knees and pray to the Lord and ask him to give you enlargement of the heart and give me $2,000."

Jesse said, "Brother Grant, why didn't you ask *me* to pray?"

"Oh," Brother Grant said, "why should I ask you to pray? You didn't offer me anything. No use of asking the Lord to give you enlargement of the heart."

Brother Knight had told him, "You can come here as often as you want, and there is a bed and breakfast for you at my home, but I'm not going to contribute to that." And he was a very generous contributor normally.

He said, "I'll tell you what I will do. I will go home tonight, and I will pray to the Lord about that. And if I get the inspiration to give you that $5,000, I'll do it."

"Well," Brother Grant said, "I might as well have the check in my pocket now. I am sure if you pray about it I'll get it."

And so, two or three days later there came through the mail two checks—one from Jesse M. Knight for $10,000, and one from Brother Smoot for $2,000.

When Brother Grant saw Jesse a few days later, he said, "What happened? I didn't ask you for $10,000. I only asked for $5,000."

Brother Knight said, "I'll tell you this, Brother Grant. When you come to me again with a mission from the President of the Church to raise funds, I'm going to pay without any question." He said, "You're much more liberal than the Lord is. I went home as I promised to do, and I told the Lord that Heber was asking me for this contribution, and I wanted to know how he felt about it. I got down on my knees, and it just kept going through my mind like a tune: 'Give Heber

$10,000.' And I got into bed and that tune kept going through my mind: 'Give Heber $10,000. Give Heber $10,000.' I got down on my knees again and said, 'Lord, Heber didn't ask me for $10,000. He only asked for $5,000.' The tune kept going through my mind. 'Give Heber $10,000. Give Heber $10,000.' And so, in order to satisfy the situation and have peace of mind, I told the Lord, 'Alright, I'll give him $10,000.' "

And so, that is what happened. This is one of the experiences of many, many that President Grant used to tell that were very interesting to me.

(Brigham Young University, *Speeches of the Year*, "Prophets of the Living God," July 29, 1969, pp. 6-7.)

JOSEPH ANDERSON

"A True Servant of God"

My acquaintance with President McKay dates back to the time before he was an apostle, when I attended the Weber Academy in Ogden. He was the principal of that school, and I a student, a country boy in short trousers. He was in my opinion the greatest teacher I have ever known. The students, girls and boys, all loved him. He was my ideal at that time, and he still is.

I recall with appreciation and satisfaction my acquaintance with him as a boy, much of the time riding horseback from Roy to Ogden over the sand ridge to get to school. I was late in starting to school because my folks were poor farmers and I had to work in the canning factory in the early fall to get means to support me in school. I recall how timid and embarrassed I was when Brother McKay called on me to come up before the class and diagram sentences and otherwise participate.

Never shall I forget him as an English teacher and particularly when we studied "The Lady of the Lake," by Scott, and "The Princess" by Tennyson. These things made such an impression on me that sixty years later, when Sister Anderson and I were in Europe on a visit, I insisted on visiting the Trossacks, the Lady of the Lake country in Scotland.

His loving, impressive personality; those eyes that look through you and search your very soul; his teachings and his example have won the hearts of millions of people—not only members of the Church but nonmembers alike. People of high and low rank who meet him—presidents of our nation and leaders of other countries over the years, men of the cloth in various churches, dignitaries, businessmen, press representatives, statesmen and politicians—all have been entranced by his great personality, his gentlemanliness, his honesty, his faith and devotion, his sense of humor, his scholarship, and his spirituality. In spite of the ailments and difficulties he has had to contend with, he never complains. His life has been and is one of service and devotion to his Church and his fellowmen. He is a true servant of God; the Lord loves him, and one cannot come into his presence without having a deep love for him and without feeling the warmth of his spirit. You cannot meet with him where matters of great importance are under consideration without recognizing his prophetic calling and his inspirational guidance.

(*Speeches of the Year*, "Prophets of the Living God," July 29, 1969, p. 9-10.)

JOSEPH ANDERSON

"Brother Grant, It's My Turn Next"

These men who stand at the head of the Church are men of destiny. It is my firm conviction that they were chosen for their work before they came here.

When President Grant was a child, playing on the floor of a building in which a Relief Society meeting was being held, Sister Eliza R. Snow spoke in tongues and Zina D. Young interpreted it. And she said that some time that little boy playing on the floor would be an apostle. Heber C. Kimball on one occasion placed Heber as a boy on a table and prophesied that some day he would be a greater man in the Church than was his father—and his father was a counselor to President Brigham Young.

Patriarch Rowberry in Tooele gave him a blessing when he was president of the Tooele Stake, and after he had concluded he said, "Heber, I dare not tell you what I saw when my hands were on your head." Brother Grant said it went through his mind as clearly as if a voice had said it: "Some day you will be the President of the Church." He said he never mentioned that to a soul until many years later when he became the President of the Church.

Patriarch Rowberry was a man who had the spirit of his patriarchal calling. I have always enjoyed this experience that President Grant told me on different occasions. Some of you may have read it.

In those days we had no automobiles, and the Brethren who went out to visit the stakes in the Church, the Brethren of the Twelve and General Authorities, sometimes spent weeks at a time visiting a stake and visiting the wards before they returned to headquarters.

On one occasion when Orson Pratt visited the Tooele

Stake, at which time President Grant was the president of the stake and Brother Rowberry was the patriarch, Patriarch Rowberry, in meeting him at the train to take him down to Tooele, said to him, "Brother Pratt. I have had a rather remarkable dream. I can't understand it. I wish you would tell me the interpretation of it."

Brother Pratt said, "Tell me the dream and I will pray about it, and if I can get the interpretation before I go back to Salt Lake I'll tell you what it is."

Brother Rowberry said, "I dreamed that I was on a big ship on the ocean, and as we traveled along the way people began to fall off that ship one after another. And finally I fell off and fell into the water and made my way to the shore. And lo and behold, when I got there I met a man." He didn't tell him his name because the man happened to be Orson Pratt himself. He said, "I met a man, and he showed me around the place where we were, whatever it was, the spirit world, I suppose. And, oh, it was such a beautiful place. Brother Pratt," he said, "this man said to me, this guide, 'Is there any place you would like to see especially?'

"I said, 'Yes, I have always had a great love for the Prophet Joseph, and I would appreciate it if I might see his home.'"

And so he showed him the Prophet's home and other places.

Brother Pratt said, "I'll pray to the Lord about it, and if I get the interpretation I'll tell you."

As Brother Rowberry was taking him to the train after his visit in the stake and visiting the wards, Brother Pratt said to him, "By the way, Brother Rowberry, I have the interpretation of that dream for you." He said, "The ship that you saw was the world, and the people who fell off were people dying, and," he said, "if you'll make a record of those who fell off the ship, in the order that you saw them fall off, as nearly as you can, they will pass away in that particular order." And he said, "When your time comes and you meet the man whom you saw in your dream, he will tell you that the dream was of the Lord and so also was the interpretation."

Some time later while President Grant was president of

the stake, Brother Rowberry came to him and said, "Brother Grant, you remember my dream. Well, I wrote down the names of those people in the order in which they fell off that ship and," he said, "they've done it. They have died just in that order."

Some time later a request came from the headquarters of the Church for the people in the stake to pray for Brother Pratt. He was very sick. They had a prayer circle room in the building where they met, and on the way up to the prayer circle room on Sunday morning Brother Rowberry said to Brother Grant, "Now, Brother Grant, you remember my dream?"

Brother Grant said, "Yes, I remember your dream."

He said, "It's all right to pray for Brother Pratt, but," he said, "it's his turn next."

Brother Pratt died on time; he didn't get well. Later, after Brother Grant became an apostle and was visiting out in Tooele, he met Brother Rowberry. Brother Rowberry reminded him of that dream and he said those people had passed away in just the order that they had been listed. And he said, "Brother Grant, it's my turn next. I just can't wait to get over on the other side to meet Brother Pratt and to meet the Prophet Joseph and your father." He said, "I'll tell them what a wonderful work you are doing as an apostle of the Lord."

The next time Brother Grant visited Grantsville, he visited Brother Rowberry's grave. That was one of the wonderful experiences that interested me, and these that I have repeated are just a few of the incidents in President Grant's life that indicated beyond a doubt that he was chosen before he came here.

(*Speeches of the Year*, "Prophets of the Living God," July 29, 1969, p. 4-6.)

Biographical Sketch

ELDER MARVIN J. ASHTON

Marvin J. Ashton, long promi-
nent in youth leadership of The Church of Jesus Christ of
Latter-day Saints, was named a member of the Council of the
Twelve in December, 1971. Previously, he was sustained as an
Assistant to the Council of the Twelve at the October 1969
general conference.

Prior to his new appointment he had served eleven
years as an assistant general superintendent of the Young
Men's Mutual Improvement Association—youth activity program of the Church—and twenty-one years as a general board
member. He is presently serving as managing director of the
Church's newly-formed Social Services Program, which includes
adoption services, Indian student placement, youth guidance,
drug and alcohol rehabilitation, and fellowshipping and rehabilitation of Latter-day Saints confined in prison. He also serves as
a member of the Board of Trustees of the Church's Health Services Corporation. In addition, Elder Ashton supervises the
Hong Kong, Philippines, Southeast Asia, and Taiwan missions.

He has directed much of his time and attention to youth
leadership. He serves presently as a national committeeman
of the Boy Scouts of America and is on the regional executive
council and the executive committee of the Great Salt Lake

Council. He holds the Silver Bear and Silver Antelope Scouting awards for outstanding service to boys and is an Eagle Scout. As an MIA executive he supervised Church-wide youth activities in music, dance, drama, speech, and athletics. For twenty-five years he supervised all-Church athletic programs.

Elder Ashton, as a Utah State senator, spearheaded legislation for improved juvenile detention facilities. In 1960 he was chairman of the leisure time division of the White House Youth Conference for the state of Utah. In addition, he serves on the Utah State Board of Alcoholism and Drugs and the board of directors of the Community Services Council.

He served a Church mission in Great Britain from 1937 to 1939 and was captain of the missionary basketball team which won the British National championship. He has traveled world-wide as a youth conference, fireside, and youth leadership director and speaker. In 1969 he was awarded the Homer 'Pug' Warner medal for outstanding service and example to youth.

Professionally, he serves as vice president of the Alta Lumber Company (a firm which he founded), president of Deseret Book Company, vice president of Dan's Food Stores, and vice president of Oneida Investment Company. He is a member of the executive committee of the Deseret Gymnasium, a member of the Salt Lake City Advisory Board of Zions First National Bank, and an official of several other business firms.

He was born in Salt Lake City May 6, 1915, a son of Marvin O. and Rae J. Ashton. He is a University of Utah graduate in business administration. Married in the Salt Lake Temple in 1940 to Norma Berntson, he is the father of four children. Mrs. Ashton is a member of the Relief Society General Board.

MARVIN J. ASHTON

"I'll Never Get in Anyone's Way"

Two weeks ago last Sunday we were in a stake conference. When it was time for the closing prayer, the stake president announced the individual's name who had been given the assignment. There were four verses in the closing song. At the beginning of the third verse I noticed a young man start from the audience, making his way to the pulpit to give the prayer. As he came toward the pulpit I noticed he was moving with a great deal of difficulty, and as he came even closer I could see that one leg was braced, heavily braced. He walked with a cane. He walked slowly. He walked with a great deal of effort as well as a great deal of courage. He barely made it to the pulpit before the song was over.

Just before he gave the benediction, the stake president nudged me and said, "This young man has just returned from the mission field." He said, "Just about two and one-half years ago he came to me after visiting with his bishop and said, 'I'd like to go on a mission. I know I have physical handicaps but I would like to go.'" The stake president hesitated, wondering what to say to the young man. Finally the young man said, to press the point, "President, if you and the bishop will let me go on a mission, I promise you one thing."

The stake president said, "What is it?"

He said, "I promise you if you'll let me go, I'll never get in anyone's way."

He went on his mission and he came back. He served in the West Central States Mission and had the opportunity of baptizing forty-seven people in the state of Montana . . . because he wouldn't get in anyone's way. A great individual.

(*Speeches of the Year*, "Murmur Not," December 9, 1969, p. 5.)

MARVIN J. ASHTON

"He Is An Old Grouch Today"

Years ago while walking with a wise friend of mine, we passed one of his neighbors as he stood in the front yard of his home. My friend greeted the man with, "How are you, Bill? It's good to see you." To this greeting, Bill didn't even look up. He didn't even respond.

"He is an old grouch today, isn't he?" I snapped.

"Oh, he is always that way," my friend responded.

"Then why are you so friendly to him?" I asked.

"Why not?" responded my mature friend. "Why should I let him decide how I am going to act?

I hope I will never forget the lesson of that evening. The important word was *act*. My friend acted toward people. Most of us react. At the time it was a strange attitude to me, because I was in grade school and following the practice of "if you speak to an acquaintance and he does not respond, that is the last time you have to bother," or "if someone shoves you on the school playground, you shove him back."

I have thought many times since this experience that many of us are perpetual reactors. We let other people determine our actions and attitudes. We let other people determine whether we will be rude or gracious, depressed or elated, critical or loyal, passive or dedicated.

Do you know people who are cool toward an acquaintance because last time they met she wasn't warm in her greeting? Do you know people who have quit praying to the Lord because he hasn't answered (so they think) their prayers of last month or last year? Do you know people who give up on others because they don't respond in the ways we think they should? Do you know people who fail to realize that Christ-like behavior patterns encourage us to be the same yesterday and forever?

The perpetual reactor is an unhappy person. His center of personal conduct is not rooted within himself, where it belongs, but in the world about him. Some of us on occasion seem to be standing on the sidelines waiting for someone to hurt, ignore, or offend us. We are perpetual reactors. What a happy day it will be when we can replace hasty reaction with patience and purposeful action.

(*Conference Report*, October 1970, pp. 36-37.)

MARVIN J. ASHTON

"A Silver Dollar in My Hand"

What a thrill it was the other day to be visiting with one of our handsome full-time Navajo

Indian missionaries when he said, "The main reason I'm on a mission today is because when I was a small boy, President Spencer W. Kimball came into our home, patted me on the head, placed a silver dollar in my hand, and said, 'Take this and start saving for a mission.'" Wrapped up in that example of leadership are all of the important parts: recognition, encouragement, challenge, and example. To bring groups back, we must learn to lead the individual back through patience and love. Good leaders don't give up. Good parents don't give up. Good youth don't give up.

(*Conference Report,* April 1970, p. 25.)

MARVIN J. ASHTON

"He's For Sale Pretty Cheap"

It is time for us to reaffirm the great truth that God's paths are straight. They not only provide safety, but they also lead to happiness and eternal progression.

Speaking of staying on the straight paths, I will never forget an experience I had with a friend in central Utah a few years ago. He had for his hobby mountain lion hunting. With other associates, dependable horses, guns, and well-trained dogs, he would seek to track the lions down, or tree them for capture. One day when I visited his place of business, he had a full-grown hunting dog tied to one of his sheds. "Isn't he a beauty!" I commented. He responded with "He's got to go. I can't be bothered with him." "What's the problem?" I continued.

"Since he was a pup, I have trained him to track lions. He

16

knows what I expect. The last time we were out on a three-day hunt, he took off after a deer, then a coyote, and finally some rabbits, and was gone the best part of a full day. He knows he must stay on the trail of the lion to be one of mine. Our business is mountain lions. Yep, he's for sale pretty cheap."

How often are we led from the right track by distractions like drugs that cross our paths? Do we sometimes seek the available "rabbit" when the big game is available up the path?

_____

(*Conference Report*, April 1971, p. 13.)

Biographical Sketch

ELDER EZRA TAFT BENSON

Member of the Council of the Twelve of The Church of Jesus Christ of Latter-day Saints since October 1943, and United States Secretary of Agriculture during the Eisenhower administration, Elder Ezra Taft Benson has served the Church in many capacities.

From 1933 to 1937, he was a member of the stake presidency of the Boise Stake in Idaho. The following year the stake was divided, and he served as president of the Boise Stake for two years. He then moved to Washington, D.C., where he became the first president of the Washington Stake, comprising all members of the Church in and immediately adjacent to the nation's capitol, which position he occupied until called to serve in the Council of the Twelve.

Elder Benson is a great-grandson of Apostle Ezra T. Benson one of the original pioneers who entered the Salt Lake Valley with Brigham Young on July 24, 1947. His parents were among the early settlers of Southern Idaho, where in the small town of Whitney he was born August 4, 1899. As a young men he was active in Scouting, priesthood work, and in the Church auxiliary organizations. He attended the Oneida Stake Academy,

Preston, Idaho and later Utah State University at Logan, Utah.

From 1921 to 1923, he served as a missionary in the British Isles. Following his return home, he continued his education at Brigham Young University at Provo, Utah, where he was graduated with honors and given a scholarship to Iowa State College at Ames, Iowa. At this institution he received his M.S. degree and was elected to the Honor Society of Agriculture. Later he did graduate work at the University of California.

From 1929 to 1930 he served as a county agricultural agent in his native Idaho and a year later was asked to head the newly organized department of agricultural economics and marketing at the University of Idaho.

He helped organize the Idaho Cooperative Council and served as its first secretary. In the spring of 1939 he received the distinct honor of being appointed executive secretary of the National Council of Farmers Cooperatives, a federation of 4,600 cooperative groups. Since then he has served on several advisory committees and national boards in the fields of agriculture and Scouting. He is a member of the National Executive Board of the Boy Scouts of America, a trustee of Brigham Young University, and a director of several commercial business firms, including C.P.C. International, which has plants in twenty-seven countries.

On January 15, 1946, he was appointed president of the European Mission of the Church with headquarters in London. The European members under local leadership had been carrying on during the war under distressing circumstances. Elder Benson was sent to attend to the spiritual affairs of the people, to reopen the missions so that active proselyting and organizational activities might be resumed, and to alleviate suffering among members by distributing food, clothing, bedding and other needed supplies sent to war-torn countries giving comfort and blessings to the people and organizing them to administer the necessary assistance. He was released from this calling on December 11, 1946.

President Dwight D. Eisenhower, recognizing Elder Benson's outstanding ability as well as his years of experience in agricultural affairs, appointed him to his cabinet as Secretary

of Agriculture in 1952. He returned to fully active Church responsibility in 1961.

In the division of responsibilities among members of the Council of the Twelve, Elder Benson supervises the Intermountain and Indian missions.

He is married to Flora Smith Amussen and is the father of six children—two sons and four daughters.

EZRA TAFT BENSON

"How Old Are You?"

There came to my office a few days ago, a fine upstanding, sweet-spirited elderly man. He came in timidly and took a chair at the desk, and then he said: "Brother Benson, how old can a man be before he is too old to go on a mission?"

And I answered: "My good brother, I do not know that there is any upper age limit."

He said: "I have been on two missions, and I would like to go on one more before I pass away. I would like to go back to Oklahoma, where I served my second mission. Do you think I am too old?"

"How old are you?"

"Eighty-six; but I would like to go once more before I die."

Now, there is much of that spirit among the priesthood of the Church. I thrill with it, my brethren, and I am grateful to be associated with men who carry that spirit.

(*Conference Report*, October 1948, p. 100.)

EZRA TAFT BENSON

"Well, What You Want Is A Returned Mormon Missionary"

. . . **M**y brothers and sisters, as I travel about the world, it is a glorious thing to note how the Church is growing and increasing. One very fine leader of a foreign state, when I asked him if there were any Mormons in his particular capital city, said: "Mr. Secretary, I have traveled a great deal, and I have come to believe that the Mormons are everywhere. Wherever I go, I find them." His statement called to mind an incident when we first moved to Washington back in 1939 or 1940. I had gone to my office early to get some work done before the telephones started ringing. I had just seated myself at the desk when the telephone rang. The man at the other end said, "I would like to have lunch with you today. I am a stranger to you, but I have something that is very urgent." I consented reluctantly, and a few hours later we faced each other across a luncheon table at a downtown hotel.

He said, "I suppose you wonder why I have invited you here." Then he added: "Last week as I came out of a luncheon meeting in Chicago, I told some of my business associates that I had been given the responsibility of coming down to Washington, D. C., to establish an office and employ a man to represent our corporation." Then he listed some of the assets in his great business organization. He said, "I began telling my associates of the kind of young man I would like to represent us in this office in Washington. First of all, I said to my associates, I wanted a man who is honest, a man of real integrity, a man who lives a clean life, who is clean morally, who, if married, is a devoted husband, and who, if unmarried, is not chasing lewd women." He said, "I would like a man who doesn't drink, and if possible I would prefer to get a man who doesn't even smoke. One of my business associates spoke up and said, 'Well, what you want is a returned Mormon missionary.' I had heard of your Church," he said. "In fact, I recall two young men in dark suits calling at our home some months ago. As I rode down here on the train last night, I decided that maybe a returned Mormon missionary was exactly what I needed. Why not? So as I registered at the hotel last night I said to the man at the desk, 'Are there any Mormons in Washington?' And the man at the desk said, 'I don't know, I suppose there are. They seem to be everywhere. But Mr. Bush, the manager, is here, and I'll ask him.' He asked Mr. Bush and gave me your name. Now that is why I have invited you here. Can you give me the names of three or four young men who meet the standards which I have just outlined?"

Well, of course it was not difficult to give him the names of three or four or a dozen who fully met the standards he outlined. I mention this, my brethren and sisters and friends, because in the Church we have certain standards—standards of living, standards of morality, standards of character which are coming to be well known to the world. These standards are admired. People with such standards are sought after. These standards are based upon true, eternal principles. They are eternal verities.

(*Conference Report,* April 1958, pp. 59-60.)

EZRA TAFT BENSON

"More Loyal Support for One Another"

. . . Some months ago while attending a meeting of agricultural and farm cooperative leaders in an eastern city, I had occasion to leave my hotel room and cross the street to the nearby post office to mail some letters. As I entered the door of the post office on a side street, I heard words coming through an open window at the opposite side of the building which sounded very much to me like a Mormon missionary preaching on the street.

After mailing the letters, I eased over to the open window, and there I saw two young men in blue serge suits standing on the corner of the steps of the post office. One young man was bearing his testimony regarding the coming forth of the Book of Mormon and the mission of the Prophet Joseph. He was earnest, he was sincere, he spoke with conviction. I thrilled with what he said. Some fifty or seventy-five people were listening in addition to the moving congregation that is always part of the street meeting. Standing at his side was his companion. In one arm were copies of the Book of Mormon, and the hats of the two brethren in his other hand.

When the street meeting ended, I went out and introduced myself, visited with them a moment, and then I turned to the young man who had been holding the literature in his arm and said, "Elder, what were you doing while your companion was preaching and bearing testimony?" The answer filled my soul with thanksgiving. He said, "Brother Benson, I was praying to God that my companion would say the right thing that would touch the hearts of the people and bring them a conviction of the truth of this great latter-day work."

Support for one another—that is the one thought that I

have to leave with you, my brethren and sisters. One of our great needs as a people is greater, more loyal support for one another.

(*Conference Report*, October 1951, pp. 154-55.)

EZRA TAFT BENSON

"A Day Which I Shall Never Forget"

My beloved brethren of the priesthood, my heart is filled to overflowing with gratitude as I look into your faces this day—a day which I shall never forget.

I am grateful beyond my power of expression for the blessings which have come to me, and particularly for this great honor that has come to one of the weakest of your number. I love this work. All my life I have had a testimony of it and a love for the leaders of the Church and for the priesthood of God. I know that it is true, and no sacrifice is too great for this wonderful work in which we are engaged.

My brethren, I must confess I had no premonition of this call, even of the shortest duration. When passing through Salt Lake and stopping here, just between trains, enroute to Colorado on the twenty-sixth of July, President McKay indicated that the President of the Church wanted to see me a few minutes. Even then such a thought as being called to this high and holy calling never entered my mind. It was only a few minutes later that President Grant took my right hand in both of his, and looked into the depths of my very soul, and said: "Brother Benson, with all my heart I congratulate you and pray God's blessings to attend you; you have been chosen as the youngest apostle of the Church."

The whole world seemed to sink. I could hardly believe it was true, that such a thing could happen; and it has been difficult since for me to realize that it is a reality.

(*Conference Report*, October 1943, p. 19.)

EZRA TAFT BENSON

"Mr. Governor, Would You Believe Such a Thing Could Happen?"

While holding a series of meetings in the eastern part of the United States a few weeks ago, I was invited by the chief executive of one of the great states to visit his office. I had no idea what he wanted to discuss, but as we sat there, it soon became clear that he was concerned with the problems of youth, and he wanted to know three things about the Mormon Church: First of all, our program of activity for youth; secondly, our great missionary system (he was not so much concerned about the proselyting program of the Church, but what that missionary system did to build character in young men); and, thirdly, the great welfare program of the Church, which tends to restore and enjoin thrift, work, and such virtues that have built this great country.

As we sat there discussing these problems, the question of family prayer came up, and he told of his experience as a boy in his own home, where he knelt in devotion each day, and then he told about visiting several of the homes of his friends recently, where there was no devotion in the home. He had great fear for the future of the youth of this great land because of the lack of spirituality in the home.

Then I had the great pleasure of telling him something of our program, and made reference to a gold and green ball which had just been held in one of the great hotels in Washington, where six to eight hundred young men and women had enjoyed themselves in an evening of sociability. There were no cigarets, no liquor, and the party was opened and closed with prayer. I said, "Mr. Governor, would you believe that such a thing could happen?"

He said: "I wish it were more common. It is almost impossible for me to believe it in view of what I know of conditions that are facing the youth of this land and what is happening in my own state."

I told him that was only typical of parties held throughout the Church. . . .

(*Conference Report,* April 1944, p. 58.)

EZRA   TAFT   BENSON

"Separation for a Period of Two Years"

I shall ever be grateful for an experience which came into our family during this latter period that I refer to, something over thirty years ago. It was during the time when sacrament meetings were held on Sunday afternoon at two o'clock, at least in the rural wards. I remember very well this particular Sunday afternoon, as father and mother returned from sacrament meeting, in the one-horse buggy. As they drove into the yard and their little brood of seven kiddies gathered around the buggy, we witnessed a thing which we had never seen before in our family. Both father and mother were in tears. We had often seen mother in tears and father offering consolation, or father weeping and mother offering sympathy. But never before had we seen them both crying at the same time. We inquired as to the reason, and we were assured that everything was all right. As we followed them into the house and sat down in the living room, mother told us that father had received a letter from Box "B." That was a call to go on a mission. She explained that they were happy; but they knew that it meant separation for a period of two years, and they had never been separated more than one night at a time in all of their married life.

This is only a little thing. Practically every family in the Church could tell similar and even more impressive experiences in connection with this great missionary movement. Father went, as your fathers and grandfathers went. The eighth member of our family was born after he got into the field. How I appreciate the faith of our mothers, and our grandmothers. Important has been their responsibility in connection with this great missionary service.

(*Conference Report*, April 1945, p. 108.)

EZRA TAFT BENSON

"That Was President Smith"

. . . My soul has been subdued and my heart made tender through the passing of our great

leader, President George Albert Smith. I have mingled feelings
of humility, sadness, and gratitude at the passing of a prophet
of God. All Israel, I am sure, has been weeping. And yet, back
of it all has been a feeling of thanksgiving for the life of this
great man. . . .

God bless the memory of President George Albert Smith. I
am grateful beyond my words of expression for the close association which I have had with him in the last few years. I am
grateful that my family has lived in the same ward and has
come under the benign influence of his sweet spirit. I shall never
cease to be grateful for the visits he made to my home while I
was serving as a humble missionary in the nations of war-torn
Europe at the end of World War II. Particularly am I thankful for a visit in the still of the night when our little one lay
at death's door. Without any announcement, President Smith
found time to come into that home and place his hands upon
the head of that little one, held in her mother's arms as she had
been for many hours, and promise her complete recovery. This
was President Smith; he always had time to help, particularly
those who were sick, those who needed him most.

(Conference Report, April 1951, pp. 45-46.)

EZRA TAFT BENSON

"They Just Stood There and Visited and Visited"

One of my non-Mormon friends
who passed away only a few days ago—who was rather promi-
nently known, who wrote for national magazines, and was chairman of the board of trustees of one of our great universities—

some months ago came to this city to address a meeting of dairymen, most of whom were members of the Church. After the meeting was over, he came up to my home for the purpose of a visit and a renewal of friendship. As I drove him back to the hotel that night, he turned to me, after being quiet for several moments, and said, "I don't know what it is, but each time I come among your people I experience something that I never experience anywhere else in the world. It's an intangible thing, but it's very real." He added, "I've tried to analyze it, I've tried to describe it, but the best thing I can do is to say that every time I come among your people, I get a spiritual uplift. What is it that gives me that feeling which I get nowhere else?"

Brethren and sisters, what is it? You feel it. We feel it in these great conferences of the Church. We feel it out in the stakes of Zion. We feel it in little branch meetings or in meetings with missionaries in the far parts of the earth. It's a sweet thing. It's a priceless thing. It is a mark of the divinity of this great work in which we are engaged.

I recall while living in the East some years ago, I invited one of my good friends, not a member of the Church, to attend our sacrament meeting. He promised that he would sometime. Weeks went by. I met him on the street one day following a Rotary luncheon, and he said, "I was up to your meeting last Sunday night, but you weren't there." I explained that I was visiting another ward, and then he said in answer to my inquiry as to whether he enjoyed the meeting, "Yes, I enjoyed it, especially the spirit of it, but," he said, "I wish you would tell me one thing. Why is it that when your people come to the end of a meeting and the benediction is said that they don't seem to have any place to go?" He said, "That group stood up, recognizing the meeting was over, but they just stood there and visited and visited until I thought I was never going to get out of that building. Finally, when I got into the foyer, it was more congested, than ever." Well, that is a further evidence of this spirit—this spirit of love, this spirit of brotherhood that is so real, my brethren and sisters, in the Church.

(*Conference Report*, October 1950, pp. 144-45.)

"Twenty-Two People Were Living in One Room"

Probably the saddest part of our mission was with our refugees. These poor, unwanted souls have been driven from their once happy homes to destinations unknown. They came with all their earthly possessions on their backs, but after organizing them into branches and calling them into meetings, they sang the songs of Zion with a fervor I am sure has never been surpassed. We visited some of their homes —their shacks—where as many as twenty-two people were living in one room—four complete families! And yet they knelt together in prayer night and morning and bore testimony to us regarding the blessings of the gospel.

Now, just a word about the Welfare Program. I bring to you, my brothers and sisters, the deep gratitude and thanksgiving of the Saints in Europe. The spirit of the Welfare Program was there long before we arrived. The Saints in various countires had sent help to their less fortunate brothers and sisters in other nations. Welfare gardens had been planted. We found them among the bombed-out buildings. We ran on to many instances where following bombings, branches had joined together and pooled all their remaining supplies, food, clothing, and household articles, and turned them over to the priesthood for distribution according to need.

It was a great joy when the welfare supplies came through. It was also a great surprise to the military authorities and others to learn with what dispatch the supplies arrived from Zion after arrangements were made and the cable sent back to Zion, March 14, 1946, to start shipments. They could hardly believe that there was a church in existence with a hundred storehouses well stocked, ready to dispatch supplies to the suffering people in Europe. You have heard figures regarding the quantities that have arrived—some fifty-one carloads. That means over two hundred European carloads, or approximately two thousand tons, and I am sure that if the cost of transporting it on the European end was considered, it would total well over three quarters of a million dollars. The bulk of that, of course, has gone to the countries in greatest distress, Germany and Austria, Holland, Norway, Belgium, with quantities going to many other countries according to need.

I have faced congregations of more than a thousand Latter-day Saints where it was estimated by the mission president that more than eighty percent of the total clothing worn was clothing from Zion, sent through the Welfare Program. My brethren and sisters, do you need any further evidence of the need for this program and the inspiration back of it? I wish you could have spent a few days with me in Europe during this past year. I tell you God is. directing this program. It is inspired! Had it not been so, there would have been many, many hundreds more of our Latter-day Saints perish with hunger and die of cold because of the lack of simple food commodities and clothing.

(*Conference Report*, April 1947, pp. 155-56.)

EZRA TAFT BENSON

"From Somewhere They Had Obtained An Old Radio"

It is quite appropriate, it seems to me, that much reference has been made in this conference to conditions in Europe and the great events that have taken place there in recent months: the dedication of the temple at Bern. . . .

Reference has been made to the European tour of the choir, the faith of the Saints, and the blessings which they enjoy today compared with only a few years ago—yes, just a short decade ago. I am very grateful to President McKay and the other members of the Presidency that Sister Benson and I were invited to attend that glorious dedication in Bern, Switzerland. I think I have never felt in all my life the veil quite so thin as it was three weeks ago this morning as we met in the opening session of that dedication service in that lovely spot in the house of the Lord, and as we listened to the prayer offered by President McKay and the remarks which preceded that prayer. . . .

Naturally I was deeply impressed with the contrast between conditions in Europe in 1946 when I was there last and conditions as we find them now. I have been going back in memory off and on ever since the dedication, reviewing in my mind the conditions that existed there when I went on an emergency mission in response to the First Presidency's call in 1946. . . .

I would like to mention this morning just one simple experience to illustrate not only the changes that have come about, but also something of the influence and the power of music and the Tabernacle Choir. . . .

. . . We were meeting at the city of Herne with the Saints of the battered Ruhr industrial area for their first district conference after the war. The meeting was being held in an old bombed-out schoolhouse. I do not recall exactly how many people were there, but there were several hundred. We had set the meeting for eleven o'clock in order to give them time to walk the long distances many of them had to come, some of them carrying babies in arms, because there were no public conveyances available and most of them had worn out their bicycles or were unable to get repair parts.

The district presidency had arranged, with our co-operation, a special surprise for the congregation that morning. From somewhere they had obtained an old radio which they had placed under cover in one corner of the building. At a certain moment in that service, which I shall never forget, the controls of that radio were turned to Radio Stuttgart, the American army radio station operated by a Mormon serviceman, and we heard strains of the Tabernacle Choir float out over the audience in that stirring and beautiful pioneer song, "Come, Come, Ye Saints."

After the second number, "O My Father," had been sung, I think there was not a dry eye among the adults in that audience. I saw before me an audience literally melted to tears through the singing of Mormon hymns by our great choir. It seemed as if all the cares of those suffering Saints were forgotten that morning. Even during the thirty-minute lunch period —when the most common item for lunch was a mixture of cracked grain and a little water such as we used to feed the baby chicks—even during the lunch period they talked of their blessings and expressed their gratitude for the gospel.

Then as we left that evening after the second session, the common expression was, as we bade them good-bye, "All is gut, Brother Benson." Well, all is good now surely. With the coming of the temples, with the material restoration that has come to those countries, and with what I hope is a deepened interest in spiritual matters—to which the temple will contribute in great measure—I hope too there will be a great increased interest in things spiritual, that those nations might be preserved in peace.

(*Conference Report*, October 1955, pp. 106-8.)

EZRA TAFT BENSON

"Many of These Saints Dressed in Rags"

To one who has spent the major part of the last year amidst the rubble and destruction of war-torn Europe, this conference has been doubly inspirational and appreciated. As I have looked into the faces of this well-fed (almost too well-fed in many cases) audience, well-clothed, surrounded with all the comforts and blessings of life, I have found that my thoughts have many times drifted across the Atlantic to those countries, and with what I hope is a deepened interest in spiritual matters—to which the temple will contribute in ren and sisters, as I am sure you do, many of you having descended through progenitors from those nations. . . .

I think I shall never forget those first meetings with the Saints. They have suffered much, my brethren and sisters. We wondered just how they would receive us, what the reaction would be. Would their hearts be filled with bitterness? Would there be hatred there? Would they have soured on the Church? I well remember our first meeting at Karlsruhe. After we had made visits through Belgium, Holland, and the Scandinavian countries, we went into occupied Germany. We finally found our way to the meeting place, a partially bombed-out building located in the interior of a block. The Saints had been in session for some two hours waiting for us, hoping that we would come because the word had reached them that we might be there for the conference. And then for the first time in my life I saw almost an entire audience in tears as we walked up onto the platform, and they realized that at last, after six or seven long years, representatives from Zion, as they put it, had finally come back to them. Then as the meeting closed, prolonged at their request, they insisted we go to the door and shake hands with each one of them as they left the bombed-out building. And we noted that many of them, after they had passed through the line, went back and came through the second and third time, so happy were they to grasp our hands. As I looked into their upturned faces—pale, thin, many of these Saints dressed in rags, some of them barefooted—I could see the light of faith in their eyes as they bore testimony to the divinity of this great latter-day work and expressed their gratitude for the blessings of the Lord.

That is what a testimony does. We saw it in many countries. I say there is no greater faith, to my knowledge, anywhere in the Church than we found among those good people in Europe.

Many interesting things happened as you can well imagine. Ofttimes our meeting rooms were in almost total darkness as we were forced to close the windows, filled with cardboard instead of glass, because of a rainstorm. But the Saints insisted that we go on with the meeting. Other times we would close a meeting, and then they would ask if we could hold another before we sent them home—they were so happy to have the opportunity of meeting with us. I remember in Nuremberg that the people had waited two hours for us—we were delayed because of detours around bombed bridges and other things. Shortly after we arrived, the curfew rang. But they requested that we allow them to stay on and after the meeting was over, they were forced to stay all night in the old partially bombed-out school-house, because of curfew restrictions. Words cannot adequately express the joy of the Saints for the first mission-wide conference following the war in England, Holland, Sweden, and other countries.

We found that our members had carried on in a marvelous way. Their faith was strong, their devotion greater, and their loyalty unsurpassed. We found very little, if any, bitterness or despair. There was a spirit of fellowship and brotherhood which had extended from one mission to the other, and as we traveled, the Saints asked us to take their greetings to their brothers and sisters in other countries although their nations had been at war only a few months before. Local missionaries had carried on during the war period. In some districts there had been more baptisms than during a comparable period prior to the war.

(*Conference Report,* April 1947, pp. 152-55.)

Biographical Sketch

BISHOP VICTOR L. BROWN

Bishop Victor L. Brown, second counselor in the Presiding Bishopric of The Church of Jesus Christ of Latter-day Saints, has had extensive experience in the Church and was an airline executive prior to his call.

Bishop Brown was born July 31, 1914, in Cardston, Alberta, Canada, a son of Gerald S. and Maggie Lee Brown. He attended the University of Utah and the Latter-day Saints Business College and has taken extension work from the University of California.

His Church activities include ward Young Men's Mutual Improvement Association superintendent, bishop of the Denver Fourth Ward, and counselor in the Denver Stake presidency for six years, from 1954 until 1960.

Bishop Brown's experience with the airlines began in Salt Lake City in 1940. He served as United Air Lines reservation manager in Washington, D.C., from 1943 until 1947, then was reservation manager in Chicago, Illinois, for one year. In 1948 he became chief of payload control at Denver, and manager of space control in 1956. He held this position for five years until he was transferred to Chicago as assistant to the director of reservations.

Bishop Brown was called to the Presiding Bishopric in October, 1961. His current Church assignments include: chairman, executive committee, Deseret Mutual Benefits Association; second vice chairman, board of trustees, Health Services Corporation of The Church of Jesus Christ of Latter-day Saints; vice chairman, General Scouting Committee of The Church of Jesus Christ of Latter-day Saints; responsibility for Church distribution and translation in seventeen languages.

He is married to the former Lois Kjar of Salt Lake City, and they have five children: Victor L., Jr.; Gerald E.; Joanne K. Soderborg; Patricia L.; and Stephen M.

VICTOR L. BROWN

"What Do You Mean, Milk?"

I was visiting with a young man one day. He is a member of a stake presidency. He was an officer in the army during the Korean War. He contemplated the possibility of becoming a professional soldier. He received a change of assignment. He knew where he was going, and he knew the reputation of his new commanding officer.

This officer was rather a wise man in some respects. He knew how to get something on the men under his direction so that he had them completely subservient to him. He was a very heavy drinker. He apparently still had some capabilities as an army officer. This young man approached this particular transfer with great concern. He wanted success, and knew he needed the recommendation of his commanding officer to achieve it.

You see, the way this officer would make his junior officers subservient to him was, when the new men came he would have a party. It would be a hard-drinking party. He would make sure that the new men drank too much. He would have women there and make sure that a compromising circumstance arose. Then he had something to hold over the heads of his men.

This young man knew that he was getting into this environment. He had already determined the kind of a person he wanted to be.

When he arrived at the party, the commanding officer said, "What will you have to drink?" "I'll have some milk, please, sir." You can imagine what happened at that. There was no milk.

"What do you mean, milk?"

"I'll have milk, please, sir."

After he had convinced the officer that he really wanted milk, someone went out and got it for him.

The pressures were on constantly to break this young man down, to make him conform to the environment he found himself in. As I indicated, he had made up his mind that he was going to be the kind of person he wanted to be, regardless of the environment.

Finally his commanding officer gave up. (Incidentally, all this time, he had worked his head off to be the best officer he could be, in every respect.) It came time for his transfer. He anticipated several demerits on his record. You can imagine his amazement when after he was transferred, his record contained the highest commendation possible from this commanding officer. He had been a nonconformist to the environment he found himself in. At the same time, he was a conformist to the standards he himself had accepted for his life.

(Speeches of the Year, "Conformity and Nonconformity," January 11, 1966, p. 4.)

"It's Serving Our Fellowmen"

Now may I share some parts of the testimony of another young marine. I do not know how old he is, but I would think if he is out of his teens, he is not far out of them. He has been a member of the Church for two years. Until recently he had been in a special reconnaissance outfit. These are men who are taken by helicopter to the far distant areas of the jungle, dropped, and told to be back at the same place in five days to be picked up.

[He said:] "I found out something that almost everybody here knows. I've only been a member of the Church two years. I didn't find this out from any member of the Church. I wasn't doing a whole lot of studying when I came over here. I was looking for the way to become active. How can I increase my knowledge of the gospel? How can the Spirit humble me more? Well, I found this out. It came to me all of a sudden. It's serving our fellowmen. It's serving the guy that sleeps next to you. It's being dedicated. There's nothing in this life that matters but that.

"It's not what kind of car you have at home. It's not how many pairs of jungle boots you got back, or what you're saving. All these little things don't matter. We didn't come to this life with these things. We came to be happy, to serve our fellowmen, to glorify God, to return to our Father in heaven. This is the key as far as I am concerned, and that is service to your fellowman. It's what's in your heart that counts, not what's on your back.

"I heard David O. McKay say that the highest ideal ever taught in any religion is service to our fellowman. This I believe with all my heart, and I know I should be thankful that Scott was baptized before he was killed, and I truly am."

Then he continued: "Brethren, I know the Church is true.

I know that this Church is divinely directed, that Joseph Smith had revelations, and that Jesus Christ is the head of the Church today. I pray that while we are over here we might strive to build our characters, to build our testimonies, that we might all do a little bit of suffering so that we might all know that joy that comes from just plain living, and that as long as our hearts are beating, and we're walking and talking, we don't have a thing to complain about, not at all."

This, then, is the testimony of a young LDS marine in South Vietnam. This is some of the spirit of our servicemen in war. After Saturday's meeting I witnessed five servicemen sharing this same spirit with five other servicemen as they took them into the waters of baptism in the South China Sea.

(*Conference Report*, October 1968, p. 120-21.)

VICTOR L. BROWN

"Sione Rose from His Knees"

Let me tell you of a young man who has felt the evidence of this love. I first met Sione in New Zealand. He is a Tongan. A finer, more clean-cut, intelligent young man I have never met anywhere. Sione comes from a very modest background—none of the luxuries and very few of the necessities. As a boy, Sione had a burning desire to obtain a college education in order to help his family as well as the Tongan people, A college education seemed totally impossible. However, one day while carrying drinking water to the men working in the taro fields, this thought came upon Sione:

"If a fourteen-year-old boy by the name of Joseph Smith could pray to God and have his prayer answered, why can't I?" So Sione dropped to his knees in the taro patch and opened his heart to his Heavenly Father and told him of his desire to become an educated person so he could improve the lot of his own people. Well, Sione rose from his knees, went about his work, returned to his home and nothing happened for a while. Then one day an enevelope came in the mail. In the envelope was the notice that Sione had received a full scholarship to the Church College of Hawaii, and he hadn't even applied for it! Now Sione had to have several hundred dollars for fare to get to Hawaii. His parents didn't have a dollar. How could he get to Hawaii and take advantage of this great blessing that had come? Well, Sione had faith, and his parents had faith, and they had works along with their faith. When the time had arrived for Sione to go to Hawaii to enter college, he had enough money to buy a one-way ticket on an airplane to get to the college.

When I met Sione he had graduated; he had his degree. He was teaching school; he was a coach, one of the most loved and respected of all the teachers in the schools in Tonga. I was talking to Sione about another assignment that would be somewhat different, an assignment whereby he would be instrumental in making the fulness of the gospel available to his people in their own tongue, in their own language, in a language where there is practically no printing of the native tongue, except, of course, in the government documents. And as Sione told me his story and as we talked, the tears coursed down his cheeks and he said, "Bishop Brown, I'll do anything my Heavenly Father wants me to do, and I'll go any place that is required." This is the result of a young man, originally in his teens, having enough faith in God to ask, knowing that his prayers would be answered.

(*Speeches of the Year*, "The Faith and Courage to Be True," May 5, 1970, pp. 6-7.)

VICTOR L. BROWN

"He Was Entranced with the Story of the Gospel"

Just about two weeks before Christmas, a companion and I boarded an airplane returning to Salt Lake City after an assignment in Mexico. My companion took the window seat and I took the aisle seat. This left an empty one between us. At the last moment we noticed a large number of servicemen being boarded. They were all sailors. A young man asked if the seat between us were available and we told him it was. He took it, and I had one of the most delightful experiences I have had for a long time.

This was a young sailor who had just finished boot camp. He was going home to Minnesota for Christmas leave. His next assignment was South Vietnam. He was one of the most refreshing young men I have met—unaffected, no pretense, friendly, warm. He was naive about travel, but, oh, how freshly naive! There was no embarrassment. He asked us if we traveled a lot, and we said we did a bit of traveling. He asked us a few things about the airplane.

As we got a little better acquainted, I asked, "Have you ever heard about the Mormon Church?"

He said, "Yes, I've heard about the Mormon Church."

I said, "Where?"

He said, "In magazines, and so on."

You know, before *I* would ask him if he would like to know more, *he* asked me to tell him about it. He beat me to the punch.

Fortunately my traveling companion was a superb missionary, formerly president of a mission. After we had talked for just a few minutes, I turned the conversation to him, because, you see, we only had a short time and he knew how to condense four or five lessons into one hour.

Victor L. Brown

This young sailor had not eaten for twenty-four hours. He had had a lot of difficulty because of weather problems in getting to Los Angeles to board his airplane, and in the last minute rush the airline had left off some meals and the servicemen weren't going to get a dinner. My traveling companion and I weren't hungry since we had eaten earlier, so I slipped my meal over to this boy and my companion slipped his meal up to this young man's sailor buddy sitting in front of us.

Then a great lesson was taught—the gospel of Jesus Christ. This sailor boy who hadn't eaten for twenty-four hours didn't eat his meal! It sat there almost untouched. He was entranced with the story of the gospel of Jesus Christ. He didn't touch his salad, he didn't touch his dessert, he didn't finish his entree. I sat there while he was being taught the gospel and I watched him. I am sure he held his fork with food on it for five minutes without even putting it down.

(Speeches of the Year, "Therefore Be Ye Also Ready," January 3, 1967, pp. 2-3.)

VICTOR L. BROWN

"Let's Let Him Make That Decision"

You might be interested in some of the programs that are going on in the Church, particularly the one that I am presently associated with—the translation of the Church program into many of the languages of the world. So if you will bear with me for a few moments, may I just tell you a little bit about this great program.

About two or two and one-half years ago, the First Presidency asked the Presiding Bishopric of the Church to establish an organization to translate, print, and distribute the Church program in Mexico and Central and South America, primarily in Spanish to begin with, and then they included Portuguese, which, of course, is the language spoken in Brazil.

Bishop Vandenberg, Presiding Bishop of the Church, asked that I assume the responsibility for this assignment. Of course, I wondered where I should start.

Any good project must be started by establishing an organization to accomplish it, so I looked for a man to work under the Presiding Bishopric's overall supervision and directly under my supervision, to head this organization. I looked widely and I talked to many people. I couldn't feel quite satisfied that I had heard the name, nor had I interviewed the man who was the one to take on this tremendous assignment.

Finally, one day in conversation with several men, the name of a man came up that I had never heard before. One of the group said, "You can't get him; he is on the road to real success in business, and you just can't touch him." I said, "Let's let *him* make that decision." So I went back to my office and placed a call to this man and asked him if he would mind coming over to my office. He said he would be happy to and was there within about ten minutes. I had spent not over two minutes talking with him when *I* knew that he was the man, and *he* knew he was the man. He expressed a willingness to assume this great responsibility.

This wonderful person, Brother J. Thomas Fyans, has been associated with me now for two and one-half or so years, and we have traveled in excess of 200,000 miles together all over the world. The Lord has magnified him greatly.

One of the most inspiring experiences of my life has been the way the Lord has opened the way for us to find the right men at the right time.

We went to Mexico City where there was a small embryo of an organization; however, it just wasn't the kind that was necessary to assume this enlarged responsibility. We talked to many people, and we almost despaired of finding the right man. You see, it is impossible for us to send men from the

United States into Mexico to manage our organizations there—they must be Mexican citizens.

As we looked, another name came to us from a conversation. I happened to have a stake conference in El Paso, Texas, and I asked this man (who lived in Pueblo, in old Mexico) to come to El Paso. He was a successful businessman, a Mexican, a wonderful person, well educated, on the road to success in his business (he was the district sales manager for a large firm). I no more than sat down with him than I knew he was the man and he knew he was the man, and he responded. Now we have an operation in Mexico that we are to be proud of—with every function performed by Mexican nationals!

Then we went to Brazil. When we left Salt Lake We didn't have the slightest idea of what to expect in Brazil and actually anticipated that we would do most of the work in Salt Lake. When we arrived at the airport in São Paulo, the mission president met us. We went to the mission home and met with the presidents of both missions in Brazil, the Brazilian South and the Brazilian Mission.

Within two hours our plan of approach was clear. We knew whom we needed to head the organization and he had agreed. He had just been offered a major position in the Mercedes-Benz agency for all of Brazil. Let me tell you just a little bit about him. He had been a Protestant minister. Just a few years ago, he was attending a seminar with other Protestant ministers. They were studying the various religions of the world. The director of the seminar called the mission home and asked the mission president to sent someone down to explain the Mormon religion. The mission president assigned a young elder to go down and explain our religious beliefs. He didn't do that. He called them all to repentance and asked them to be baptized.

This really struck one or two of them as being rather bold and strange. This good man, Helio Camargo, decided that there must be something about this religion if a young man just in his teens (or just out of his teens) would have the courage to approach a group of ministers that way. He started to quietly investigate to see what caused and motivated this young man to have much courage. He started to study the gospel. He is a very intelligent man, a graduate of the West Point of Brazil. He began a principle at a time. He studied each one in depth, and as he became converted to that principle, he started to live it. This man started to pay his tithing six months before he was baptized because he had studied the law of tithing and had become converted to it. Then, after studying other principles of the gospel, he was baptized. Now he is our manager in São Paulo, Brazil, and he is a bishop in the Church in the first stake organized in South America.

Shortly after we had received the assignment for Latin America, we were given the same assignment for the European languages. This is when we met President and Sister Dean Peterson in Oslo.

One of our key men in Europe came from Gratz, Austria. He has an interesting background both inside and outside the Church. He had only been a member of the Church about six years. This man is of noble birth. The missionaries called at his home. He wasn't home. His wife told them to come back. When he came home and she informed him of the appointment, he told her that he would throw them out. She asked him to be a little more gentle than that. The appointment was for two o'clock in the afternoon. Right on the dot of two o'clock, two missionaries came to the door. One of them had a frayed shirt collar. This man thought to himself, if these young men are that devoted and this one is apparently of quite humble circumstances, then I guess I ought to be courteous enough to listen to them. So he invited them to come in and they started to teach the gospel to him.

He said, "No, I don't want that. I want you to answer some questions."

I only remember two or three of the questions, but there were about five or six. Now this is from a man who was a very devout Catholic.

"Does your church preach infant baptism?"

"Does your church preach that the family will live together after death?"

"Does your church treat the wealthy any different than they treat the poor?"

Of course the missionaries answered these questions.

Then he said, "This is all I need to know—I am ready for baptism!"

He has excellent facility with five languages. He can, as I recall, use another four or five languages. He has said that he is sure that all of the training he went through during his early life was to accomplish the work he is doing now, in helping to translate the gospel of Jesus Christ into his mother tongue.

I could go on and on, relating experiences of these wonderful people whom the Lord has raised up. Then He made it possible for us to find them and to find them at the proper time.

(*BYU Summer Devotional*, "To Every Tongue and People," June 20, 1967, pp. 3-6.)

Biographical Sketch

ELDER   MATTHEW   COWLEY

Recorded in the journal of Sister Abbie Hyde Cowley is the following: "Monday morning at 3:00 a.m., August 2, 1897, I gave birth to a fine boy weighing 8½ lbs. Sister Swan and Brother and Sister Hale were present, and by the blessing of the Lord, I was safely delivered, for which I am ever grateful to our Heavenly Father." Thus is recorded, in the words of his mother, the birth of Matthew Cowley. His father, Matthias Cowley was a member of the Quorum of the Twelve.

In 1914, while Matthew was attending the LDS University in Salt Lake City, he received a call to serve as a missionary in the New Zealand Mission. When he arrived in New Zealand, he was still only seventeen years of age, but because of his pleasing disposition and great ability, he soon won the hearts of the Maori people of that mission. He became fluent in the use of the Maori language. At the conclusion of the normal three-year mission period, he received a special call from President Joseph F. Smith, President of the Church, to remain in New Zealand long enough to translate the Doctrine and Covenants and Pearl of Great Price into the Maori language, and also to revise and re-edit the previous translation of the Book of Mormon.

In 1919, after completing five years as a missionary, he returned to his home in Salt Lake City. When he returned home, he resumed his education. Through the efforts of friends, he was allowed to enter the University of Utah to begin his study of law. While attending the University of Utah, he was employed at the Federal Reserve Bank in Salt Lake City, and after completing one year of study at the university, he was admitted to the law school of George Washington University in Washington, D. C.

He attended school nights and worked in the Federal Reserve Bank for a while during the daytime. He later was employed by Senator Reed Smoot as a special assistant to the Senate Finance Committee, and continued in this service until he graduated and returned home. He began his law career upon his return in 1926 and was shortly thereafter appointed deputy Salt Lake County attorney. After two years as a deputy, he was elected to fill the office of county attorney. At the conclusion of this term, he returned to private practice until 1938, when he was called by the First Presidency to preside over the New Zealand Mission.

On July 13, 1922 while still studying in Washington, D. C., he returned home to be married in the Salt Lake Temple to Elva Eleanor Taylor. Their marriage was performed by President George Albert Smith, then a member of the Council of the Twelve.

On October 5, 1945, Brother Cowley was sustained a member of the Council of the Twelve as the Church met in solemn assembly in its semi-annual conference. In this conference, President George Albert Smith was sustained as the President of the Church, and his first call to the apostleship went to this young man whom he had guided and loved since early childhood.

On October 11, 1945, Elder Cowley was ordained an apostle, the sixty-fifth of this dispensation, by President Smith. Approximately a year later, a new position of responsibility among the General Authorities of the Church was created, and Elder

Cowley was appointed to fill the position as President of the Pacific Islands Missions. In this new assignment, he was given the responsibility of directing the affairs of the Church in the many missions of the Pacific. His headquarters in this assignment continued to be in Salt Lake City, but during the following three years, he traveled almost continuously in the islands of the sea. The entire Polynesian people now had the opportunity of being blessed by him as had the Maori people during the thirteen years that he had lived with them as missionary and president.

He had a great gift of language and was able to speak in the native tongue so that he could be understood by the people in all his travels. In addition to his travels in the islands, he visited in the missions of the Orient and in Australia. He visited the Philippine Islands, Japan, and China, dedicating China once again for the preaching of the gospel. After approximately three years in this special assignment, he was released, and from then until his death, he traveled extensively along with the other General Authorities visiting the stakes and the missions of the Church.

At the time of his passing on December 13, 1953, he had become one of the most loved men of his time. Few men have ever been so greatly loved and so greatly respected. He affected the lives of everyone who knew him.

(*Matthew Cowley Speaks,* [Salt Lake City: Deseret Book Co., 1971], pp. vii-xii.)

MATTHEW COWLEY

"Oneness of Direction"

I was in a home recently in one of our stakes where a man was lying upon his bed. The only parts of his body that he could move were his eyes and his tongue. He could speak and he could see, but that was all; no life in his arms, no life in his legs. The home was immaculate, his bed linen was immaculate, he was immaculate. Maybe there was no life in his hands, but his companion held that hand in a grasp as strong as life itself. The clasp of the hand, brothers and sisters—it has meaning! And when you are away from one another, if you don't feel a spiritual clasp stronger than the physical clasp, rush back to one another as quickly as you can. You know true love is not looking at each other in one of these old-fashioned loveseats—looking into each other's eyes. That isn't true love. True love is that love which comes into your heart and motivates your life when you arise from the altar and both of you look in the same direction, down through eternity. That is true love, where both are looking in the same direction.

The Maori in referring to his wife says: "Taku hoa wahine."

That means, "My companion wife." The wife, in speaking of her companion, says: "Toku hoa tane—My companion husband." I like that a little better than just saying "my wife," or "my husband."

"My companion wife," "My companion husband!" Companionship implies a oneness of direction, right down through eternity.

(Conference Report, October 3, 1952, p. 28.)

MATTHEW COWLEY

"We Are Fasting and Praying"

I had an experience down here about fasting.

I have got two friends down here from New Zealand—a couple. They had never had any children, and they finally thought they had adopted one, but one day along came the father and said he wanted his child. Maybe you saw it in the newspaper. It was in the headlines covering quite a period of time. He said, "I never put that child in that home to be adopted, just to be cared for." He had two other children. His wife was a drunkard, and she left him and left the children. "Now she is back with me. She has reformed. We want our children back." This couple had one of them. Well, they had had that child so long it was one of the family, and so they had a long drawn-out litigation.

I was there at conference a couple of months ago. This couple was here. They came up after one of the meetings on

Sunday. I said, "How is the case coming out? What is happening?"

They said, "Well, the final hearing is on Tuesday."

I said, "All right. Tomorrow morning I have an engagement for breakfast. After that I will fast all day Monday until Tuesday evening. You join me. We will fast for that child, and then whatever happens is right." So they shed a few tears and we fasted, and I never heard any more about it until general conference. The lawyer was at conference.

I said, "How did the case come out?"

He said, "Well, it was the strangest thing. I called the witness to take the witness stand, and I said, 'You tell the judge now what you are doing for this child, what kind of home you have, what its prospects are for the future, the husband's ability to care for it, his job, the money he is making, and everything.' That's what I intended her to say. But I said, 'Tell the court what you are doing for this child.' Do you know what she said? She said, 'We are fasting and praying.' Do you know what the judge did. He had to declare a recess. He didn't say a word. He went back in his chambers and spent a few minutes, and he came out, and he awarded this child to these two, this couple. They have been married in the temple and had it sealed to them."

(Address at San Fernando Stake welfare meeting, Mary 24, 1952.)

MATTHEW COWLEY

"I'm Ready Now to Bless Your Boy"

We have a mutual friend down in Honolulu, Sister Widstoe and I, a man who is a young bishop down there, very wealthy, and yet a young man with a lot of humility. He was called one day from the Queen's Hospital to come and bless a boy who had polio. A native sister had called him. He was her bishop, and she said, "Bishop, come up here, my boy is stricken with polio, and I want you to come up here and administer to him and bless him." All day she waited for him, and the bishop never showed up. All night he never showed up. The next morning he never showed up, but early in the afternoon here he came. She turned loose on him. She called him everything she could think of. "You, my bishop, I call you and tell you my boy is here stricken with polio. And you your own boss. You have your cars, you have a beautiful yacht, you have everything you want; and your time is your own; and you don't show up. You just come now after a whole day."

After she had finished and couldn't think of anything more to call him, he smiled and said, "Well, after I hung up the receiver yesterday, I started to fast, and I've been fasting and praying for twenty-four hours. I'm ready now to bless your boy." At five o'clock that evening the boy was released from the hospital, entirely cured of his polio. ". . . This kind goeth not out but by prayer and fasting."

(*Matthew Cowley Speaks*, [Salt Lake City: Deseret Book Co., 1954], pp. 149-50.)

MATTHEW COWLEY

"What on Earth Will I Do?"

When I was invited to come here, President Wilkinson suggested that I might talk a little bit about miracles. Well, it will be a miracle if I do. I had a particular assignment or instruction from President George Albert Smith when I was called to this position. He called me into his office one day and took hold of my hand, and while he was holding my hand and looking at me he said, "I want to say something to you, Brother Cowley."

I said, "Well, I'm willing to listen."

"This is just a particular suggestion to you, not to all the brethren but to you." He said, "Never write a sermon. Never write down what you are going to say."

I said, "What on earth will I do?"

He said, "You tell the people what the Lord wants you to tell them while you are standing on your feet."

I said, "That certainly is putting some responsibility on the Lord."

But I've tried to live up to that instruction. And I've had some great experiences.

(*Speeches of the Year,* "Miracles," February 18, 1953, p. 2.)

MATTHEW COWLEY

"Secretary of the Relief Society"

I am personally grateful for the confidence this Church had in me in my extreme youth. I was just turning seventeen when I was called to go to New Zealand as a missionary. My first appointment there was to a little place called Judea, a wonderful place to go, for a young missionary. At the first meeting I attended in Judea, I could not understand the words that were being said, and after the meeting a sister who could speak English said to me: "Do you know what they said in here, and what they did?" I said, "I could not understand a word."

She said: "Well, you were called and sustained as the secretary of the Relief Society of the Judea Branch."

I made up my mind right there and then that the Relief Society was not going to take any liberty with my time as a missionary without my knowing something about it; and so I determined to get the gift of the Maori language, even if I had to work for it. And I did have to work for it.

I studied eleven hours every day for several weeks. I read the Book of Mormon in Maori, and my studies were punctuated with fasting and with prayer. And on my twelfth Sunday I delivered my first sermon in the Maori language. They do speak with new tongues, those who accept the call to the ministry of our Lord and Savior Jesus Christ.

(*Conference Report*, October 1948, p. 156.)

MATTHEW COWLEY

"He Was An Unusual Boy"

A few weeks ago I was called to the County Hospital in Salt Lake City by a mother. I didn't know her. She said her boy was dying from polio and asked if I would come down and give that boy a blessing. So I picked up a young bishop whom I generally take with me, for I think his faith is greater than mine, and I always like him along.

We went down there, and here was this young lad in an iron lung, unconscious, his face rather a blackish color, with a tube in his throat; and they said he had a tube lower down in his abdomen. He had been flown in from an outlying community. The mother said to me, "This is an unusual boy. Not because he's my child, but he is an unusual boy." I think he was eight or nine years of age.

After they put the usual coverings on us, we went in, and we blessed that boy. It was one of those occasions when I knew as I laid my hands upon that lad that he was an unusual boy, and he had faith. Having faith in his faith, I blessed him to get well and promised him he would. I never heard any more about him until last Sunday. I was on my way to Murray to conference; I dropped in the County Hospital, and I asked if I might see the lad. The nurse said, "Certainly. Walk right down the hall." As I walked down the hall, out came the boy running to meet me. He ran up and asked, "Are you Brother Cowley?"

And I said, "Yes."

He said, "I want to thank you for that prayer." He added, "I was unconscious then, wasn't I?"

I replied, "You certainly were."

He said, "That's the reason I don't recognize you." Then he asked, "Come in my room; I want to talk to you." He was an unusual boy. Well, we went in the room. He still had a tube in his throat. I said, "How long are you going to have that tube there?"

He said, "Oh, two weeks. Two more weeks, and then I'm all well. How about another blessing?"

So I said, "Certainly." I blessed him again. I was in a hurry. I wanted to get out to my conference. But he stopped me and asked, "Hey, how about my partner in the next bed?" There was a young fellow about sixteen or seventeen.

I said, "What do you mean?"

He said, "Don't go without blessing him. He's my partner."

I said, "Sure." Then I asked the boy, "Would you like a blessing?"

He said, "Yes, sir. I'm a teacher in the Aaronic Priesthood in my ward." I blessed him, and then my little friend went and brought another fellow in. Here was another partner. And I blessed him.

Now, except ye believe as a child, you can't receive these blessings.

(*Speeches of the Year*, "Miracles," February 18, 1953, pp. 2-3.)

MATTHEW COWLEY

"Fix Me Up, I Want to Go Home"

I know one of our dearest friends in New Zealand who is now reaching the end of his life; he's only two years older than I, and it's entirely due to his eating habits. He owned a taxicab company out there in one of the cities; every cab in the town he owned. One day he was stricken and started to have a hemorrhage from the nose, which couldn't be stopped. So they took him to the hospital, and the doctors couldn't stop it. So they sent for his family, and they came to be there when he passed on. When the family was standing around and the nurses were still working on him, he said to one of the nurses, "You go to the phone, and call my switchboard at the taxi office, and tell the girl to send a couple of my drivers out here quick." Every driver of every cab he owned was an elder in the Church.

The nurse went to the switchboard and called her and said, "The big man wants you to send a couple of his drivers out here to the hospital fast." She knew what it meant, so out went two drivers. "Fix me up, I want to go home," Just like that you know. One anointed him, the other sealed the anointing, and he got up out of bed and went home. The hermorrhage had ceased immediately. It was the simplest thing in the world, wasn't it? He didn't have any doubt at all about the power of God to heal. Medicine had failed, medical science had failed, so with simple faith he had his taxi drivers bless him.

(*Matthew Cowley Speaks*, p. 148.)

MATTHEW COWLEY

"Just As Miraculous As Raising the Dead"

A little child who lives on "B" Street was hit by an automobile, down in American Fork. For seven months that child lay on that bed up there at home. It never spoke; it was unconscious, had to be fed intravenously. I was speaking down in the old Granite Tabernacle, for a Japanese girl's farewell. The girl was a hairdresser, and the mother of this child was one of her clients. So after the meeting, she came up and said to me, "I wonder if you would have time to come up and bless my little girl?" I said, "Yes, I would be glad to; where do you live?" She told me, and I said, "That's not far from where I live."

So the next day we went up. I called a young bishop and away we went. We went up there and saw this child. Now, I believe if I hadn't been among the natives down in the islands, I wouldn't have had a bit of faith. There was that child helpless, all crippled up. And after that I went up once in a great while; once or twice I went fasting. One day I picked up the telephone at home, and the mother said to me, "Just wait a minute." So I waited there a minute, and I heard a little voice say, "This is so and so." And it was that little girl.

Last summer she was baptized, and she asked me if I would baptize her. So I went down to the Tabernacle and baptized the little girl. Now she is going to school. Her vision isn't perfect yet, but it is coming back. She is walking, and she is playing. Now to me that was just as miraculous as raising the dead.

(*Matthew Cowley Speaks*, pp. 150-51.)

MATTHEW COWLEY

"The Doctor Isn't Home"

When I went over to New Zealand on my first mission, I had only been there a day or two when a nice sister came running to me. And she said, "Come over, please." I was all alone. I didn't have a companion. I went over to the home, and there was a little boy, ten or eleven, I guess. He had fallen from a tree. She said, "Fix him up." I said, "You ought to have a doctor." I had never administered to anybody in my life, never. She said, "The doctor isn't home. He is away from town. We don't need a doctor. You fix him."

Well, I got down. He lay on the floor. I anointed him, and I sealed the anointing. You know, I guess God wanted to humble me. The next day he was climbing trees again. Every bone had knit. It was only a few days after that that her husband was stricken with typhoid fever. I was scared to death. The water was bad. I was all alone, just a youngster. She called me into her husband. I got down and anointed and blessed him, and the next morning he came over to my house and visited with me. And he said, "If you are going anywhere now, you can go. I am well." I have never had experiences like that in all my life.

(Address delivered at San Fernando Stake conference, May 28, 1952.)

MATTHEW COWLEY

"I Can't Say That About My Church"

I stand up here and I say, "Brothers and sisters, I know that this is the true Church." I said that once in a little village outside of Honolulu. Sitting down in front of me was an army officer. He was a member of the Church. He had a beautiful wife. She was sitting there. She was not a member of the Church. I said, "I know that this is the true Church. If there is anyone here who doesn't belong to this Church, no matter what church he belongs to, I hope that he doesn't think I am depriving him of the right to stand up and say that he knows he belongs to the right church. I will have all the respect in the world for him if he has that conviction."

After that meeting this colonel came up to me and said, "You have just converted my wife. The only thing that has kept her out of the Church is because we are such braggers. We are always saying, 'We know we have the true Church,' and when you told her she could get up and say the same thing about her church, right after the meeting, she said to me, 'I can't say that about my church. I will have to join.' "

(*Matthew Cowley Speaks*, pp. 328-29.)

MATTHEW COWLEY

"They Fed the Lovely Parents"

 I was in Canada one day about five years ago. And I went to a home of a bishop for dinner. He wanted me to stay at his home, but he didn't have room. Well, I went to dinner. When the dinner was all set he went into a little room and carried out a little woman—a lovely little soul, with white hair—and he took her over and placed her down gently in a chair at the table. Then he took a serviette and put it around her neck, pushed the chair up close. And then he went back to the room and came out with his arms around an elderly man—a little white-haired man—and then he took him over and gently placed him at the side of the woman. Then he took a serviette and put it around his neck. And then we all sat down.

And then he said, "Brother Cowley, this is the reason we don't have room for you. These are the parents of my wife, and we're trying to get even with them, while they're so helpless, for what they did for my wife when she was a helpless child." And before that man and his wife took a spoonful of food, they fed the lovely parents, who couldn't feed themselves. "Woman, behold thy son; son, behold thy mother." Did you ever hear anything more beautiful than that?

(*Leadership Week Lectures, 1953*, "Learning to Live through Better Use of Vocational Opportunities," June 19, 1953, p. 4.)

MATTHEW COWLEY

"The Mortgage Is Paid Off"

Over in Colorado once, I was at stake conference, and I asked one of the elders quorum presidents how his elders were getting along as a quorum. I said, "Do you do anything to help one another?"

"Oh, yes, we don't do bad."

I said, "Well, what are you doing?"

He said, "Well, I can tell you this: we've got a member of our quorum in the hospital down in Santa Fe, New Mexico. He was a strong, vigorous young man, buying a beautiful farm—a hard worker with a lovely little family. He was going ahead, paying off his bills and his mortgage, when all of a sudden he was stricken." Ordinarily that would have been the end of the farm, the end of security of the family. The elders quorum president said to me, "That was our loss as much as it was a loss for his wife and children. So we took over, and we've gone out and operated that farm. It doesn't take much time with all of our tractors and all our equipment. The mortgage is paid off, and the family has a good income from the farm. All the man has to worry about is getting well, down there in that hospital."

(*Leadership Week Lectures, 1953,* "Learning to Live through Better Use of Vocational Opportunities," June 19, 1953, p. 5.)

MATTHEW COWLEY

"You Do Not Owe That Much Tithing"

I had a little mother, and I still have her, down in New Zealand. I knew her on my first mission when I was just a young boy. In those days she called me her son. When I went back to preside, she called me her father.

Now, on one occasion I called in, as I always did when I visited that vicinity, to see this grand little woman, then in her eighties and blind. She did not live in an organized branch, had no contact with the priesthood except as the missionaries visited there. We had no missionaries in those days. They were away at war.

I went in and greeted her in the Maori fashion. She was out in her back yard by her little fire. I reached forth my hand to shake hands with her, and I was going to rub noses with her. And she said, "Do not shake hands with me, Father."

I said, "Oh, that is clean dirt on your hands. I am willing to shake hands with you. I am glad to. I want to."

She said: "Not yet." Then she got on her hands and knees and crawled over to her little house. At the corner of the house there was a spade. She lifted up that spade and crawled off in another direction, measuring the distance she went. She finally arrived at a spot and started digging down into the soil with that spade. It finally struck something hard. She took out the soil with her hands and lifted out a fruit jar. She opened that fruit jar and reached down in it, took something out and handed it to me, and it turned out to be New Zealand money. In American money it would have been equivalent to one hundred dollars.

She said. "There is my tithing. Now I can shake hands with the priesthood of God."

I said. "You do not owe that much tithing."

She said. "I know it. I do not owe it now, but I am paying

some in advance, for I do not know when the priesthood of God will get around this way again."

(*Conference Report*, October, 1948, pp. 159-60.)

MATTHEW COWLEY

"Then I Am Safe for Another Week"

We had a young sailor who came into our home in New Zealand during the war. He was a convert to the Church. Before he left San Francisco, he had been ordained a priest. And we asked him about his life on board ship. He was the only member of the Church on this big transport.

He said, "Well, whenever we stop at a port, the fellows all come around and kid me and say, 'Come on, let's go out and have a good time, get on a binge, get some relaxation.' But I do not go. You know the reason I do not go? You know the reason I can stand up against those invitations and temptation?" He said, "It is because the captain on the ship on Sunday gives me a little room, and I go into that little room all by myself. I have that little serviceman's copy of the Book of Mormon, so I take a little water and a piece of bread. I open up that Book of Mormon to Moroni, and I get down on my knees. I bless the sacrament, and I pass it to myself." And he said, "Then I am safe for another week." He said, "Nobody on earth can tempt me." He was learning how to live, fast, but not learning fast living. Just remember, he was learning to live the simple life.

(*Leadership Week Lectures,* June 19, 1953.)

MATTHEW COWLEY

"I Walked Fearlessly"

I was called to faraway New Zealand, and in that mission I was assigned, without a companion, to one of the most humble places I have ever seen in all my life, one of the most poverty-stricken places. And in that little village, I had to pray. I was there but a few days when a woman came rushing to my room, and I have a picture of that room—no floor, just the ground with a woven mat and a blanket or two. She came rushing to that room and asked me to arise from my bed and hurry to her little hut. And when I arrived there, I found her companion lying on the ground, being consumed by the fire of typhoid fever. All I could do was pray; and I knelt beside that suffering native, and I prayed to God and opened up my heart to him. And I believe the channel was open. And then I placed my hands upon that good brother; and with the authority of the priesthood which I as a young boy held, I blessed him to be restored to health. The next morning the wife came again to my room and said, "If you have anywhere you desire to go, you are now free to go; my husband is up."

I remember that on another occasion I rode horseback all day long and far into the night to arrive at a native village

74

on the seacoast of New Zealand. And when I arrived at a bay dividing the place where I had to stop at that little village, I made a fire so that the people across in the village would send a rowboat to get me. And when that boat arrived, I was taken across the bay, and I walked through that village, and in every home there were cases of typhoid fever. But I walked fearlessly, with my head erect, impelled by the priesthood of God which I held. And in each of those homes I left the blessings of heaven. And I laid my hands upon the sick. And then I had to go across the bay again and get on my horse and ride all night long to arrive at another native village where there was sickness.

(*Conference Report,* October, 1953, p. 107.)

MATTHEW COWLEY

"See What You Have Done For Me"

I was down in the Southwest Indian Mission. I went into church one day, and a fine-looking Navajo woman came in. And the missionary said to me, "I want to introduce you to this sister." So he took me up and introduced me to her, and we had a little chat, the best we could. Then after meeting this young missionary came to me and said, "Well, I am glad you met her. A few months ago my companion and I went to the Navajo reservation. We went into a hogan. There lay this woman on her back—on a sheepskin. She had been there for six long years. She had never stood up. When we were about to leave, she said to us, 'Isn't there something you people do for people who are sick and afflicted?' I said, 'Yes.' She said, 'Will you please do it for me?' So we got down on

75

our knees; one anointed her with oil, the other one sealed the anointing. After we left—we were only a short distance away —she came running out from the hogan and said, 'Come back and see what you have done for me.' She has been walking ever since."

(*Speeches of the Year*, "Miracles," February 18, 1953, p. 10.)

MATTHEW COWLEY

"That One Day Was Spent in the Temple"

I had a brother called in the first war. He was in Washington at school when he was called. My father had the idea that he should go to the temple and receive his blessings before he went overseas. Next door to us lived President Anthon H. Lund, counselor to the President of the Church. My father went over and talked to him and said, "I certainly would like to see my boy come home to receive the blessings of the temple before he goes overseas." President Lund said, "Why not? You know how to do it." My father knew what he meant, and he prayed, and President Lund helped him. In three or four days my father received a wire from my brother that said, "Our captain here has passed away. He is from San Diego. I have been appointed to escort the body to San Diego, and on my return I will pass through Salt Lake City, and I will be there for one day." That one day was spent in the temple.

(*Matthew Cowley Speaks*, pp. 381-82.)

MATTHEW COWLEY

"She's Physically Well from Head to Foot"

I went into a hospital one day in New Zealand to bless a woman who didn't belong to the Church. She was dying. We all knew she was dying. Even the doctor said so. She was having her farewell party. Ah, that's one thing I like about the natives. When you go, they give you a farewell party. They all gather around. They send messages over to the other side. "When you get over there, tell my mother I'm trying to do my best; I'm not so good, but I'm trying. Tell her to have a good room fixed for me when I get over there—plenty of fish, good meals." My, it's wonderful how they send you off. Well, there they were, all gathered around this poor sister. She was about to be confined, and the doctor told her it would kill her. She was tubercular from head to foot. I had with me an old native, almost ninety. She was his niece. He stood up at the head of the bed, and he said, "Vera, you're dead. You're dead because the doctor says you're dead. You're on your way out. I've been to you, your home, your people, my relatives. I'm the only one that has joined the Church. None of you has ever listened to me. You're dead now; you're going to live." He turned to me and said, "Is it all right if we kneel down and pray?"

I said, "Yes." So we knelt down. Everybody around there knelt down. And after the prayer we blessed her. The last time I was in New Zealand she had her fifth child, and she's physically well from head to foot. She has not joined the Church yet. That's the next miracle I'm waiting for.

(*Speeches of the Year*, "Miracles," February 18, 1953, pp. 8-9.)

MATTHEW COWLEY

"I Received a Message"

I've learned a lot from these islanders that I see scattered around here. I see Albert Whaanga from New Zealand in the audience; I wish he'd teach you people how to rub noses. That's what we do down in New Zealand, you know. We don't really rub. You just press your forehead and your nose against the nose and forehead of the other person. It's a wonderful thing. You can always tell when they're keeping the Word of Wisdom down there. All you have to do is walk up and greet them and sniff a little bit, and you've got 'em! It would be a good practice to have over here. . . . So if I ever come up to one of you some day and say I'd like to rub noses with you, you'll know I'm suspecting something.

These natives live close to God. They have some kind of power. I guess it's just because they accept miracles as a matter of course. They never doubt anything. They used to scare me. Someone would come up and say, "Brother Cowley, I've had a dream about you."

I'd say, "Don't tell me. I don't want to hear about it."

"Oh, it was a good one."

"All right. Tell me."

And they'd tell me something. Now I remember when President Rufus K. Hardy of the First Council of the Seventy passed away. I was walking along the street of one of the cities in New Zealand, and one of our native members came up—a lady.

She said to me, "President Hardy is dead."

I said, "Is that so? Have you received a wire?"

She said, "No. I received a message, but I haven't received any wire." She repeated, "He's dead. I know."

Well, I always believed them when they told me those things. When I got back to headquarters, I wasn't there long when here came a cablegram which said that President Hardy had passed away the night before. But she knew that without any cablegram. She told me about it.

I got out of my car once in the city. I got out to do some window-shopping to get a little rest from driving. I walked around, and finally I went around a corner, and there stood a native woman and her daughter. The mother said to the daughter, "What did I tell you?"

I said, "What's going on here?"

The daughter said, "Mother said if we'd stand here for fifteen minutes you'd come around the corner." Now she didn't have any radio set with her, just one in her heart where she received the impression.

After President Hardy died, we had a memorial service for him. I'll never forget the native who was up speaking, saying what a calamity it was to the mission to lose this great New Zealand missionary who could do so much for them as one of the Authorities of the Church. He was talking along that line, and all of a sudden he stopped and looked around at me and said, "Wait a minute. There's nothing to worry about. When President Cowley gets home, he'll fill the first vacancy in the Council of the Twelve Apostles, and we'll still have a representative among the Authorities of the Church." Then he went on talking about President Hardy. When I arrived home the following September, I filled the first vacancy in the Quorum of the Twelve. Now did that just happen by chance?

(*Speeches of the Year*, "Miracles," February 18, 1953, p. 7.)

MATTHEW COWLEY

"Medical Science Had Laid the Burden Down"

A little over a year ago a couple came into my office carrying a little boy. The father said to me, "My wife and I have been fasting for two days, and we've brought our little boy up for a blessing. You are the one we've been sent to."

I said, "What's the matter with him?"

They said he was born blind, deaf, and dumb, had no co-ordination of his muscles, couldn't even crawl at the age of five years. I said to myself, this is it. I had implicit faith in the fasting and the prayers of those parents. I blessed the child, and a few weeks later I received a letter: "Brother Cowley, we wish you could see our little boy now. He's crawling. When we throw a ball across the floor, he races after it on his hands and knees. He can see. When we clap our hands over his head, he jumps. He can hear." Medical science had laid the burden down. God had taken over. The little boy was rapidly recovering, or really getting what he'd never had.

(*Speeches of the Year*, "Miracles," February 18, 1953, p. 8.)

MATTHEW COWLEY

"Send for the Elders"

I was called to a home in a little village in New Zealand one day. There the Relief Society sisters were preparing the body of one of our Saints. They had placed his body in front of the Big House, as they call it, the house where the people came to wail and weep and mourn over the dead, when in rushed the dead man's brother.

He said, "Administer to him."

And the young natives said, "Why, you shouldn't do that; he's dead."

"You do it!"

This [was the] same old man that I had with me when his niece was so ill was there. The younger native got down on his knees, and he anointed the dead man. Then this great old sage got down and blessed him and commanded him to rise. You should have seen the Relief Society sisters scatter. And he sat up, and he said, "Send for the elders; I don't feel very well." Now, of course, all of that was just psychological effect on that dead man. Wonderful, isn't it—this psychological effect business? Well, we told him he had just been administered to, and he said: "Oh, that was it." He said, "I was dead. I could feel life coming back into me just like a blanket unrolling." Now, he outlived the brother that came in and told us to administer to him.

_____

(*Speeches of the Year*, "Miracles," February 18, 1953, p. 9.)

_____

MATTHEW COWLEY

_____

"Give Him His Vision"

I've told the story about the little baby nine months old who was born blind. The father came up with him one Sunday and said, "Brother Cowley, our baby hasn't been blessed yet; we'd like you to bless him."

I said, "Why have you waited so long?"

"Oh, we just didn't get around to it."

Now, that's the native way; I like that. Just don't get around to doing things! Why not live and enjoy it? I said, "All right, what's the name?" So he told me the name, and I was just going to start when he said, "By the way, give him his vision when you give him a name. He was born blind." Well, it shocked me, but then I said to myself, why not? Christ told his disciples when he left them they could work miracles. And I had faith in that father's faith. After I gave that child its name, I finally got around to giving it its vision. That boy's about twelve years old now. The last time I was back there I was afraid to inquire about him. I was sure he had gone blind again. That's the way my faith works sometimes. So I asked the branch president about him. And he said, "Brother Cowley, the worst thing you ever did was to bless that child to receive his vision. He's the meanest kid in the neighborhood, always getting into mischief." Boy, I was thrilled about that kid getting into mischief!

(*Speeches of the Year,* "Miracles," February 18, 1953, pp. 9-10.)

Biographical Sketch

Loren C. Dunn, appointed to the First Council of Seventy of The Church of Jesus Christ of Latter-day Saints in 1968, has been named supervisor of missions in the British Isles. He is also an associate member of the Missionary Committee of the Church.

At the time of his appointment in 1968, Elder Dunn was living in Natick, Massachusetts, and was director of communications for the New England Council for Economic Development, with headquarters in Boston. He was also secretary of the council's banking and finance committee.

Elder Dunn was born in Tooele, Utah, on June 12, 1930, a son of the late Alex F. Dunn and Carol Horsfall Dunn. His father was president of the Tooele Stake of the Church and publisher of the *Tooele Transcript Bulletin*.

Elder Dunn was married in the Salt Lake Temple on December 15, 1959, to Sharon Longden of Salt Lake City, Utah, a daughter of the late Elder John Longden, Assistant to the Council of the Twelve, and LaRue C. Longden. The Dunns have three children.

He was graduated from Brigham Young University in 1953

with a BS degree in journalism. While at BYU he was a member of the basketball team which in 1951 won the Western States Conference championship and went on to win the National Invitation Tournament title. This team also toured South America.

From 1958 to 1961 Elder Dunn was editor of the *Tooele Transcript*. He then went on to Boston University where he received a MS degree in public relations. In 1962 he was assistant director of public relations for the *Herald Tribune* Fresh Air Fund in New York City. While in Boston he had articles published by *Public Relations Journal* and by the *American Banker*.

Elder Dunn was in the U.S. Army in Europe from 1956 to 1958. He was a director-elect of the Boston Rotary Club, and is currently a member of the Salt Lake Rotary Club. He was also a member of the Public Relations Society of America, the New England Press Association, and is active in Scouting at the council and regional level.

Elder Dunn was chairman of a special committee named by the governor to establish an industrial development information system for Utah. He is on the board of directors of Pro-Utah. He also is a member of the Utah Industrial Promotion Board.

His Church activities began with a proselyting mission to Australia in 1954-56, where he was a counselor to the mission president. He was group leader for Mormon servicemen in Aschauffenburg, Germany, then an Explorer post advisor in Tooele before going to New England. He was superintendent of the New England Mission Mutual Improvement Association before being made a counselor in the presidency.

Mrs. Dunn was Young Women's Mutual Improvement Association president in the Boston Stake and served in the stake Primary presidency. She was graduated from the University of Utah in 1958.

LOREN C. DUNN

"When We Recognize the Priesthood"

Shortly after being called in April Conference just two years ago, I returned to Boston to get my personal affairs in order so that I could make a permanent move to Salt Lake City. I was released from the New England Mission presidency, and for the first time in five years had more opportunity to attend my own ward in the Boston Stake, since I was usually traveling on mission business every weekend. I can remember going to our ward and, incidentally, if you want to see a picture of frustration, you should see a bishop in whose ward there is a General Authority with no assignment! I went to my own ward and I was invited to sit on the stand, which I did. A counselor in the bishopric was conducting the meeting, and he said these words, and they will forever be in my mind: "Presiding at this meeting is Brother Loren C. Dunn of the First Council of the Seventy, and the meeting will proceed under his direction." Now, I didn't have anything to do with the meeting other than just being there and being a member of the First Council of the Seventy. Yet above me and behind me, I felt a force that came down through me and from me out to the audience, and

I was given to know that this was a manifestation of the Spirit of the Lord that made itself manifest because the presiding authority had been recognized.

Now, don't get me wrong, I am not talking about Loren C. Dunn. He will go along, and some day he will pass from the scene and turn to dust and be forgotten. He is not very important really, but the mantle and priesthood and authority that have been conferred upon him *are extremely important* and this is what the Lord, I am sure, was trying to tell me. When we recognize the priesthood, when we recognize presiding authority, the Spirit of the Lord begins to operate.

(*Speeches of the Year*, "Establish Divine Communication," March 24, 1970, p. 6.)

LOREN C. DUNN

"Who Is Going to Care?"

I remember a story told by a forest ranger about a tourist coming to a national park to take pictures of wildlife. Not far from the campground he found what he was looking for—twin bear cubs rummaging around in a garbage dump, half playing, half looking for dinner. Grabbing his camera, he proceeded to take a series of pictures from a number of different angles. In his haste, he failed to realize that when you find bear cubs in the forest, the mother bear is never very far away.

As he moved to get a close-up shot of the playful cubs, he inadvertently came between the cubs and the mother bear, who was in the trees a short distance off. The bear struck out immediately for her cubs, and a near disaster was averted when a passerby, noticing the scene, alerted the tourist, who demonstrated unusual athletic ability as he vacated the garbage pit.

We often hear of the ferocity with which animals protect their young, and usually these stories are associated with incidents about parents who for some unexplainable reason abandon their children. While these actions can and should be condemned, nonetheless, we seem to live in a day and age where there is another kind of abandonment, which is almost worse than a mother leaving an unwanted baby on a doorstep.

What I am talking about is the temptation of parents to give up on their children, especially when those children seem to flaunt and disregard the laws of morality and conduct which the parents hold dear and which govern the home, and when the children seem to rebel against every effort parents make to correct their behavior or show them a better way.

At least a baby who has been left on a doorstep will be looked after by the appropriate agencies, and usually placed in a home where parents who want it will adopt it and love it and raise it as their own.

A boy or a girl who has been given up by his or her parents because they (the children) are off on the wrong foot and possibly even surly and rebellious to any parental effort is in a much more serious predicament. When the hard times come —and they will—who is going to care if the parents don't?

(*Conference Report*, October 1970, pp. 41-42.)

LOREN C. DUNN

"My Father Never Gave Up On Me"

I had a young girl come in to see me the other day, a beautiful girl, neat and clean, giving a good appearance. But the story she told was anything but clean, and far from beautiful.

From her early teenage years, she had become involved in drugs. It became so bad that at one time in her life she had moved away from her family and was more or less drifting from one pot party to another. She had taken up the so-called hippie culture and was high on drugs most of the time.

"Strangely enough," she says, "during all this time my father never gave up on me, and although I knew I was breaking my parents' hearts, I could always go home to my father and know that he loved me, and that he wouldn't condemn me as an individual, although he condemned everything that I did."

This girl went on to say that one night she had what she called a bad trip; I believe she referred to it as "freaking out." She said it was such a terrifying experience that she went home to her parents and spent the rest of the night in bed with them, just as she must have done as a child when she had a nightmare. She had no real rest until her father finally gave her a blessing, which seemed to ease her mental and physical torture.

This happened to be the turning point in this girl's life. She said she always knew it was wrong but was just determined to rebel. Bit by bit she has now put her life back together again, and although she still has a way to go, she is going to make it now.

She had a father, you see, who never gave up on her.

(*Conference Report*, October 1970, pp. 42-43.)

LOREN C. DUNN

"One Electrifying Moment"

I recall a stage play that recently was made into a movie. It dealt with parents whose only child, a son, returned from military service. The father and son had never been close. It was a situation in which both father and son loved each other but were unable to find ways to express themselves, and therefore hostilities arose because each thought the other did not like him. It was a breakdown of communication.

But now the son was home from the army, and things were different. The father and son began to establish a whole new relationship. The high point of the play came when the boy said to his father something like this:

"Dad, I always resented you when I was younger because you never told me that you loved me, but then I realized that I had never told you that I loved you either. Well, Dad, I'm telling you now: I love you."

For one electrifying moment the father and son embraced each other as the pent-up love and appreciation of years came flooding out. This probably would never have happened had the son not realized that he was as guilty of lack of expression as his parents.

(*Conference Report,* April 1969, pp. 22-23.)

LOREN C. DUNN

"To Me, This Is the Generation Gap"

My grandparents came over from Kirkintilloch, Scotland. They settled out in Tooele. At the tender age of sixty Grandfather started a newspaper, and when he got to be about eighty years old, my father began to help him in the business. Because Grandfather had particular ideas as to how things should be run, there were differences of opinion. My father was trying to introduce new machinery and new innovations into the business, but Grandfather just couln't see it. And this led to some rather interesting discussions as only it can between Scotchmen. I didn't know my grandfather, but my father tells of having a particularly stimulating discussion with him one day when Grandfather suddenly turned to him and said, "Now, Son, why can ye no be like me? Why can ye no be agreeable?"

My father passed away about five years ago. He was a very innovative man. He introduced some important concepts that strengthened our business and caused it to grow. But then my brother came along—the third generation—and he had still newer and more innovative ideas, some of which I don't think my father completely grasped because, you see, they were two different generations. There wasn't the difficulty between my brother and my father that there was between my father and my grandfather because greater understanding existed.

Well, my brother now heads the business, and he has introduced the computer and other innovations; but I suspect in a few years hence one of his boys will come up and say, "Now, Dad, there is a better way, and there is an easier way," and I suspect that if dad is like the rest of us he will say, "Now wait a minute, Son." And there might be a little debate about what is good and what is bad.

To me, this is the generation gap. It has always existed

Loren Charles Dunn

and always will. But I do think in light of this, that the younger generation has the greater responsibility. The younger generation is usually more flexible and because of this has a greater responsibility to close the generation gap—perhaps even a greater responsibility than the older generation.

I suspect that you can be more successful in trying to understand what the older generation is saying to you and what they mean than possibly they can in trying to understand what you mean. This modern world as it stands today in all its innovation and advanced science and technology would make it harder for them, I think, to come to a complete understanding of your point of view than it would be for you to reach out and try to find meaning in what they are trying to say. Try to keep this in mind as you seek to establish communication with those you consider your elders.

(*Speeches of the Year*, "The Need to Know," April 1, 1969, p. 5-6.)

LOREN C. DUNN

"Splinters of Glass"

We have a three-year-old daughter whom we love very dearly. Not long ago I was doing some studying at my desk at home, and she was in the room playing with a glass of water that was on the desk. As she picked up that large glass with her little fingers, I repeatedly warned her that she must be careful or she would drop the glass, which, of course, she finally did. It shattered as it hit the floor, and splinters went in every direction.

Showing the patience of a wise parent, I immediately spanked her, explaining to her that the spanking was the consequence of her insisting on not listening to me by picking up the glass until it dropped and was broken. She shed some tears and gave me a hug, which she usually does when she knows she is in trouble, and the event was quickly forgotten.

Since she often plays in her bare feet, I took her out of the room and made every effort to sweep up all the glass particles. But the thought came to me that perhaps I hadn't gotten all the splinters of glass, and at some future time when she is playing in that room, those little feet might find the splinters which went undetected, and she would have to suffer anew for that which she did.

For a young person to violate the law of chastity or some other commandment and then to later put his or her life in order—such action, I am sure, will mean the forgiveness of an understanding and loving God. Yet as that person progresses in life and reaches a point where he or she enters into a marriage contract and as they have children of their own, it just might be that a splinter of a previous wrongdoing somewhere on the floor of his or her life might prick the conscience."

(*Conference Report*, October 1969, pp. 13-14.)

LOREN C. DUNN

"I Had Made The Wrong Decision"

I can remember a few years ago when I had a critical decision to make, while we were still living in the East. I had an important job offer made to me and I went through all of the steps that we have talked about here, made a decision to the best of my ability, then contacted the people and turned them down. The next twelve hours I went through almost a "hell," before I realized that the Lord was trying to tell me I had made the wrong decision. Interestingly enough, the people whom I had turned down called me again and upped their offer—I would have been more than happy to settle for whatever they offered me in the first place!

(*Speeches of the Year,* "Establish Divine Communication," March 24, 1970.)

LOREN C. DUNN

"We Will Be Spiritually Dead"

While thinking of what I might discuss with you this morning, there were certain conversations I have had in my life which came to mind. There are some people, I believe, who raise the question from time to time, "When should we listen to a prophet?" or, "When *doesn't* a person speak under the inspiration of the Spirit?" This causes me to reflect on a story I heard as a boy about a man who set out to break his chickens of the habit of eating, figuring that he could save a great deal of money if he could accomplish this feat. But just as he had broken them of the habit they up and died on him. I think to some extent this is what happens to the thinking of some people in the Church of Jesus Christ, when they try to shut off the sources of revelation. I believe our conversation and our thinking should be more in line with, "What are the ways through which the Lord can communicate with us?" and not, "When does a person speak under inspiration?" I believe that if we take the negative approach, sooner or later we will reach the point where we will have shut off all the spiritual food and, indeed, we will be spiritually dead.

(*Speeches of the Year,* "Establish Divine Communication," March 24, 1970, p. 2.)

LOREN C. DUNN

"Clinging to A Fence"

Perhaps you remember a story that took place a few months ago. It appeared in most of the newspapers. A little girl was found clinging to a fence that divides a super freeway in one of the world's largest cities. The police were summoned, and as they brought the girl to safety, she unfolded this pathetic story.

It was her parents, you see, who put her there. They had said, "Now hang on to the fence and don't let go for any reason." Then the parents drove off, planning to desert her. The newspaper account was graphic. You could picture the little girl, a tear in her eye, lower lip quivering, but holding fast to the rail as cars and huge trucks went roaring by on each side, not daring to let go because daddy had told her to hold on— standing there determined, waiting patiently, for a mother and father who never intended to return.

(*Conference Report,* October, 1970, p. 43.)

Biographical Sketch

PRESIDENT PAUL H. DUNN

Elder Paul H. Dunn, a career church educator and author, was named a member of the First Council of Seventy April 6, 1964, during the 134th Annual General Conference of The Church of Jesus Christ of Latter-day Saints in Salt Lake City, Utah. He has served as president of the New England Mission with headquarters in Cambridge, Mass.

Elder Dunn was born in Provo, Utah, April 24, 1924, a son of Joshua Harold and Geneve Roberts Dunn. He was married to Jeanne Alice Cheverton on February 27, 1946. They are the parents of three daughters, Janet Dunn Gough, Marsha Jeanne Dunn Winget, and Kellie Colleen.

He was graduated from Chapman College with an A. B. degree in religion in 1953, and received the M. S. degree in educational administration in 1954 at the University of Southern California. He received his doctorate in the same field at U.S.C. in 1959.

Dr. Dunn is the author of three books: *You Too Can Teach*, *Ten Most Wanted Men*, and *Meaningful Living*.

Elder Dunn served as coordinator of LDS Institutes of

Religion in Southern California for two years prior to his call to the First Council of Seventy. He began his association with the Church's educational system in 1952 as a seminary teacher in Los Angeles.

An outstanding school athlete, Elder Dunn participated in baseball, football, basketball, golf, and track, and played professional baseball for four years before resuming his educational career.

PAUL H. DUNN

"His Name Was Lou Gehrig"

Going back to when most of you were still in the pre-existance, I suppose awaiting your chance to come here, Brother Dunn, at the age of thirteen, was anxiously trying to get involved in the career of being a ball player; and you know you have to start early in any profession. I started when I was in the crib. I was throwing the rattle back and forth and causing a little commotion and finally graduated to the play pen and other things. Finally, because of sheer perseverance, I got to be a bat boy for the Little Rock Travelers down in Arkansas. They were a local AA team. That doesn't mean much to you sisters, but it was a pretty active ball club that did a lot to prepare young men for the major leagues. To be a bat boy was not only wonderful because of its environment, but it had many fringe benefits, one of which was to get personally acquainted with all the players. Then, in the spring, the frosting—because the major league clubs would come through Little Rock, as they do now in Arizona, Florida, and California, and other states in the South where the warm weather occurs a little bit earlier than it does in the north; and they take on these local teams.

Well, during the late thirties, my idol of a team was the New York Yankees. I guess it was with most people. I have changed a number of times since, but among all of the players that made up that powerful row of pitchers and sluggers was the player of my life, who unfortunately passed away before most of you were born. You may have heard of him. His name was Lou Gehrig, and he became the symbol of everything good and wonderful in the world to me. I patterned my whole life after him. He had more influence on me than Mom, Dad, Sunday School, and priesthood leader all rolled into one, because sometimes people do this to you. It's wonderful and I think all the more reason we need to select proper idols. But I didn't have much sense or vision at the time. Fortunately, Gehrig was a great soul, a great Christian, a great leader. Being the bat boy on the field, I got personally acquainted with him. One day I walked up to him and I said, "Mr. Gehrig, I wonder if you would help me."

Here is the difference between the great person and average person. He slipped his arm around me. Most people don't have time for kids, pests at that; and believe me, I was a pest. I just followed him around like a shadow. He put his arm around me and said, "What can I do, Paul, to help you?"

I said, "Mr. Gehrig, I want to be a ball player."

He said, "That's fine. I think you will if you have the desire and the determination and you continually prepare yourself."

I said, "Well, that's just my problem. I want it more than anything else; but every time I walk out on the ball field, I get so scared I can hardly perform." (You know the butterflys; you almost want to quit before you start. You get it occasionally up here, don't you? Whenever you go to perform.) And I said, "Can you help me?"

He patted me on the towhead, and he said, "Don't you ever lose that fear, Paul. Don't you ever lose it." (Watch this teacher at work now.) He said, "Fear's good, but you need to learn to control it; don't lose it."

I thought, now that's strange from a great ball player; and I said, "Why is that?"

He said, "Because fear is there, I think, for a purpose." (That's Gehrig talking.) He continued, "You know, for what it's worth, today in this practice game, I'm just as frightened at the plate as I was the first day I walked out on the field. The difference is, I control it; I discipline it." I thought, well, that's interesting; you never looked very scared to me. He said, "Paul, when I come out of the dugout, because I feel this way, I'm reminded of two things, and this is why fear is good: I'm reminded that there is a higher source than me, and I've got to depend on it. I can't do it alone." (Too many people try to go it alone in this old world, don't they?) He continued, "So, I bring Him into my confidence and I get strength and direction. Then I am reminded that there are eight other ball players on the field." (Get that young people, because sometimes leaders-to-be think that they have to do it alone. No, the thing that made Gehrig great was that he was an all-team man.) And he said, "I need the other eight in order to erform properly."

Well, I asked him the next question which I think might have entered your mind: "That's wonderful, Mr. Gehrig; but how in the world do you control it? It's got me all over. Now, how do I discipline it?"

He didn't answer me. He said, "Let me think about it."

The day ended, still no answer; but the next day—the great teacher at work. I'm out shagging balls (that's picking up balls ladies) behind old Red Ruffing. This name won't mean much to some of you, but he is still existing and has been considered for the Hall of Fame. A great big old 220 pound, red-headed pitcher who was pretty uncouth and had a vocabulary you didn't want to share with thirteen-year-olds; but there I was listening to it. I was handing him the balls so he wouldn't have to stoop over as he was throwing in to the players in batting practice. Here came Lou Gehrig, about the fifth or sixth guy to take his spot in the batting cage; and before he stepped into the arena, as it were, he called out, "Hey, Red, let the kid pitch to me." (Gasp!) I thought, me pitch to him, the greatest man in my life? Red didn't want to bother. See the difference in people? He said, "I haven't got time; I want to get through with my warm-ups and go take my shower."

Gehrig, who was normally a very calm, understanding soul, just raised his voice a little. He said, "I said, let the kid pitch to me!"

He said, "All right, here."

Well, when I stepped up on that mound, that ball, nine ounces, felt like a shot-put. I thought, how do you do it? When I threw the first one, I think it bounced about four feet out. Finally, the ball got a little bit closer, and he called out words of comfort and encouragement. After about the fifth pitch, I got it reasonably close where he could take a swing at it. With a little more comfort and counsel from him, I got the ball into where he hit one or two. Then about five or six pitches later he took one of the healthiest cuts I have ever seen him take, even in a pro game. Oh, did he have the wrist action and the powerful swing! He came on so fast the breeze would blow your head off. But he missed the pitch. Then he stood straight up in that batter's box; and he said, "Nice shot, Paul." Boy, I thought, look out world! I had just thrown that ball right by the greatest hitter in the game. Do you know what that did to my faith, to my confidence? And, I didn't have sense enough at thirteen to know that maybe he missed it on purpose. He might just have done that. Well, he missed another one or two in the process; and to keep me humble—that's always important isn't it, in this old world—he hit a couple out that haven't landed yet, that are still in orbit.

After he had finished his practice, he called me off the mound. He said, "Come here a minute." And then slipping that great, wonderful arm around me, he walked me over to the dugout. He said, "Paul, (I thought this was an interesting observation) you've got a lot to learn about the game yet."

"Yes, I suppose you can say that."

He said, "You know (here is the key, young people), for a boy thirteen, you have fantastic control. Keep working on it, and you will go all the way."

You know, I worked on that for the next five years without letting up because one man said, here's one little quality, Paul. You've got plenty of limitations. You've got more errors than perhaps good in you, but here's something that's strong in you. You capitalize on it. This is how you get the confidence and the faith, and discipline the fear; you start where you are strong. Always pick the strength, young people, and use it to overcome the limitations. That is all this great leader was telling me.

PAUL H. DUNN

"A Standing Ovation"

I had an opportunity, just a few months ago, to be a representative of yours at Boston College, one of the great institutions in the East. While on that campus, I had an opportunity to meet one of the distinguished cardinals from another faith. He was a very fascinating giant of a man, in his own right. He is not known to smile very much, however, and I thought, here is the supreme test. So as we were introduced, I was presented to him as the head of the Mormon Church in the New England area. I tried to qualify that, so I said, "No, sir, I'm a cardinal myself." He said, "You are?" I said, "Yes sir." He said, "I didn't think they had the position of cardinal in the Mormon Church." I said, "They don't. I played for St. Louis." Well, he almost smiled.

While there, it was my honor, along with two of my elders, to go before a very challenging class in religious education. A great number of the students were preparing for the ministry. It was fascinating to me to place my two assistants at the head of the class as we were given the time to talk about our faith. I might just say in preface that, prior to going over, I had received a call from the father in question when I first arrived in New England. We chatted about the niceties of the great country to which we were both assigned, and finally he said, "Dr. Dunn, would you come over and tell us about your faith?" I said, "Thank you for the honor. If I might speak very frankly, I don't know that you want me under the conditions that I am committed to come. So I'll tell you. I have been sent here by a prophet of the Lord, and I'll tell you as delicately as I know how that you're wrong and we're right. And if I did come, it would be on the basis of declaring the error of your faith and announcing the truth. I've worked for our Church on many campuses throughout the country, and I know that probably very little good will come from my visit other than you'll be more convinced you're right and I'll go away convinced I'm right. Now I have been sent for three years to call your people to repentance." "Thank you for your honesty," he answered, and we hung up.

Six months ago, he called again. "This is Father So-and-So; do you remember?"

"Yes, I remember our coversation," I said.

"I'd like to have you come and talk to my class," he remarked. "We have many that will be ordained to the ministry shortly."

I said, "Do you remember the qualifications I set down before?"

"Yes. We'd like to have you on that basis."

I said, "Fine, I'm your man." And so I took my two elders and went over.

When we got there, the class looked interested, and I had my two assistants stand and speak for about five minutes each. I do not think the importance of what they said was quite as great as what they radiated. They were twenty-one-year-old boys who had left their homes to come and preach the gospel of Jesus Christ; the Spirit was evident. As my first assistant started to speak, the first cigarette went out, then the second. The audience started to sit more erect in their tablet armchairs, and they listened. And then it came my turn, and after joking with them for a few moments and trying to create a proper rapport, I took from my pocket the thirteen Articles of Faith, and read each one in turn, giving a little two-minute dissertation on each. As you know, you must be rather sensitive when you are talking with an all-Catholic audience. I concluded by bearing solemn witness and testimony to this Church. And then it happened. It was almost as if a baton in the hand of a choir director had been set up as a signal. The class arose in unison and, for about two minutes, gave three Mormon elders a standing ovation. We found out a little later why. One by one, as they approached the front of the room taking each one of us by the hand, the comment was:

Thank God there are some people in the world that won't compromise.

(*Speeches of the Year*, "Be Not Ashamed," September 29, 1970, pp. 4-5.)

PAUL   H.   DUNN

"Now If You Want An Interview, Listen"

Billy Casper came to town for the Avco Classic. He wanted to know if we could get together about some missionary business. I was honored and went out as his special guest to the country club. Because he had shot the worst round in his professional career on that very course one year before, he came back to take revenge. And as you know, he won that classic by a stroke or two. During the great event that was staged at Sutton, Massachusetts, he invited me as his spiritual caddy. I know what a spiritual divot is now. As we came back into the clubhouse after his first round, I tried to beg off and say, "Well, now, I'd better leave you alone." "No, you come in here," he would reply. The reporters just mobbed him. We got back in a private section of the clubhouse where the big stars were lockered, and every reporter from any major newspaper in Massachusetts now had him surrounded. You know what they wanted to talk about—golf, golf, golf. But Billy is not ashamed of who he is or what he represents. So he said, "No, we're not going to talk about golf right now, I've brought another man and he's going to talk to you." He said, "This is President Dunn of the New England Mission." "Well, what's that?" they asked. "He's going to talk to you about it." So for quite a while we sat in the seclusion of the clubhouse and talked about things that matter most, and the reporters were fascinated. For the first ten minutes they tried to get back to golf, but Billy said, "Now if you want an interview, listen." So they listened. It was great and exciting.

(*Speeches of the Year,* "Be Not Ashamed," September 29, 1970, pp. 3-4.)

PAUL H. DUNN

"I Was a New Board Member"

I had one other introduction that was rather interesting. I think I have shared this with some of you. I used to live in Hollywood, California. I moved from there with my good family when the children commenced to outnumber the facilities. I hadn't been in my new stake more than a few hours when the stake president called and, as they often do, enlisted me in a new assignment. I was assigned to the stake Sunday School board. And very quickly I was turned over to the stake superintendent who gave me two assignments for the following week. Well, there I was, in a whole new area. I didn't know anybody or any place. But trying to be dutiful to my calling I went to the ward I thought was my assignment. (I later found that there were two wards on the same street, in different parts of the stake.)

I walked in—I thought on time, but found I was tardy by about fifteen minutes—and as fate would have it, there wasn't a seat left in the congregation. So what do you do?—a new board member on assignment, no seat in the audience. I thought, "I'll take my place on the stand." Well, I wasn't too diplomatic, and I walked up while a man was talking. It embarrassed him, so he stopped and watched me come up. I hurried and took my seat, bowed my head so the pressure would be elsewhere. Then he said something, about three minutes later, that told me I was in the wrong ward.

"Oh, good heavens," I thought. "What do you do now? I need to make my report. I've got to go visit the other ward." Then it struck me that I had one thing in my favor. Nobody knew me—here I was a new board member, new stake—so I quickly got up and walked out. The same fellow was still talking. You can imagine how my leaving must have built his confidence. I was never so glad to get outside in all my life. I hurried on, and found the right ward, and completed my assignment.

The following Tuesday we had a stake Sunday School board meeting. I went to report. The superintendent was so excited when I walked in, he grabbed me.

He said, "Do you know what happened in our stake?"

"No, what happened?"

"Well, last Sunday we had a spiritual experience we'll always remember."

"Oh! What was that?"

He said, "Do you know that at Blank Ward (the ward I had walked into first) they had a visit from one of the Three Nephites!"

I want to assure you this morning I'm not here in either capacity. But I am honored to be here.

(*Speeches of the Year*, "Know Thyself, Control Thyself, Give Thyself," October 7, 1969, pp. 6-7.)

PAUL H. DUNN

"Where Do You Sign Up?"

I had a little girl down at the University of Southern California. (I think it is long ago enough so that you wouldn't identify her as your first cousin or somebody else's.) She came from a wonderful, typical Latter-day Saint home, her father was in a very responsible position. But like lots of young people who go away from home, she thought she would take the proverbial Roman holiday, and so she signed on her religious preference card, "Protestant," instead of standing up to be counted and signing it "Latter-day Saint." She thought she would get away for a little breather.

She was rushed by one of the very fashionable sororities at the university and it was about a month later before I learned from another Latter-day Saint student that she was even on campus. So I went to pay her a visit. That was my charge—I was supposedly the shepherd and this was one of my little lambs. So I went to pay her a call. She was living at a big, fancy sorority house on 28th Street in Los Angeles. It was lavishly furnished, with a big, curling, beautifully decorated staircase. I rang the bell, and the chimes sounded all over the place. I was ushered in, and she was summoned. I will never forget that experience. Little Jan descended the stairway holding in her hand a long cigarette holder, and attached to it was a long king-size cigarette.

She was very proud and flip about it, and as she came into my presence, she said in a very sophisticated voice, "Yeaaa-s?"

I said, "Jan, I'm Brother Paul Dunn, your institute director."

"Oh," she said, "I've had enough church," and she took a big puff and blew the smoke back in my face.

It was all I could do to hold my patience. But I mustered up courage, girded up my loins, looked at her, and I said, "Just so you will know, Jan, we have a wonderful program here. I have been commissioned by the Lord through his prophets to be your caretaker. I want you to know that we need you, and I think you need us."

"No," she said, "thank you anyway, I've had enough church. In fact, I'd appreciate it if you wouldn't bother me. Take my name off your records."

Well, I couldn't do that, because I knew of her capacity in becoming a true daughter of the Lord. So I commenced to work out a plan in my mind for her.

Fortunately she was in a four-year program, and every week for the next four years she either saw me, got a telephone call, or a letter. I used to pull her card—I had access to it from the dean's file, being the campus chaplain for the Latter-day Saints—and I would find out what building and what time she was in a particular class. Then I would just "happen" to be there when class let out. We'd bump into each other. I'd say, "Jan! How are you?"

"Oh, you again?"

"Why don't you come on over? We're having a great time."

"No, thank you anyway, Brother Dunn, but I just can't work you in—can't find the time—too busy." (What an excuse that is, "too busy.")

Well, to make a long story short, four years came and

went. Then in the last semester of the fourth year a knock came at my door at the institute. I opened it, and in the framework stood Jan. For a moment I was speechless. Then I said, "I'm honored, Jan, that you'd come."

"I thought you might be." She said, "Where do you sign up?"

I said, "Are you serious?"

"Yes, sir."

I said, "May I ask just what motivated you to take a class?"

She said, "Very simple. I thought it was easier to sign up for a class and get you off my back."

I was flattered. She took a class.

A year and a half later an interesting event transpired. Brother Dunn was called to Salt Lake. Jan had met a wonderful dental student in our program, and a call came on the phone one day, "Brother Dunn, would you honor us with your presence in the temple?"

"I'd be honored, Jan."

And that wonderful day arrived. Kneeling across the holy altar in one of our sealing rooms in the Salt Lake Temple was this little former dental hygienist and a great young man who had all that any girl would desire, holding hands. And by the authority of the Holy Melchizedek Priesthood, I had the sacred privilege of uniting that pair for time and all eternity.

As I felt the Holy Spirit come, I couldn't help but reflect back on that day so many years before, when she had descended the stairway and in that rather sophisticated sort of fashion, said, "Yeaaa-s, what may I do for you?" The very scene before me was what I had desired for her.

_____

(*Speeches of the Year*, "Know Thyself, Control Thyself, Give Thyself," October 7, 1969, pp. 11-12.)

_____

"Two Can Play This Game"

I appreciate, President Lewis, your gracious introduction today. I have thought of one or two unique introductions I have had. I don't know, it might be appropriate to share them with you. Brother Lewis indicated that I was at one time associated with the institute program in Southern California. In that particular position you often have a chance to visit with dignitaries and just people in general. We were in the process of doing some remodeling in our institute building on one occasion, and I was entertaining some bids from very important establishments. I had an appointment this one morning with a representative from one of the better-known firms. And right at ten o'clock, the appointed hour, a knock came at my door. I opened it and standing in the framework was a very interesting looking character. He still had his hat on, even though he was in the building. His tie and shirt had parted company and from the aroma that came from him, I could tell that he had just disposed of a Roi-tan before coming in. I could handle all that. It was his announcement that challenged me.

He said good morning with all the firmness I have ever seen in a man. He took me by the hand. He said, "My name is Joseph Smith."

Well, now, I don't know what your concept of the Prophet is, but mine was not this. And you know your mind will do a hundred and one things when startled. I was startled.

I thought, "Now what is he up to? Joseph Smith, Mormon Church, kind of a cocky character." I thought, "Two can play this game." So I just squared my shoulders and put out my chin and said, "I'm glad to meet you, Joseph. I am Brigham Young."

He really looked shocked. And then he gave me shock

number two. He reached in his pocket, pulled out a business card. The firm I was expecting was represented, and his name was really Joseph Smith! By then I didn't have the heart to tell him that I wasn't Brigham Young. And so all during the conversation he kept saying, "Yes, Mr. Young. Thank you, Mr. Young." I can imagine what he must have told his cronies back at the office.

(*Speeches of the Year*, "Know Thyself, Control Thyself, Give Thyself," October 7, 1969, pp. 5-6.)

PAUL H. DUNN

"A Tiny Speck of Dirt"

This summer I made a trip through Arizona and California. While driving with my family across the desert and enjoying every minute of the trip, even though it was quite warm, I suddenly became conscious of the fact that my car had lost all of its power. For a few moments it coasted, and then at a very slight rise in the road it stopped dead still. I looked at the gas gauge and discovered that I had plenty of fuel; the radiator temperature was normal; the oil level was all right; and the fan belt was still in place. So I knew that the trouble was not in an overheated engine. And knowing my mechanical aptitude, I knew I was in for a short hike. A friendly traveler took me to a phone a couple of miles up the grade; I called a mechanic and then had to walk back two miles to the car. The mechanic arrived and almost immediately sensed the difficulty; he stuck the end of a very tiny pin through a hole in one of the parts in the engine, and the car was ready to go again. A tiny speck of dirt, so small that it could hardly be seen by the naked eye, yet sufficient to stop the progress of five people for two hours, caused one of us to walk two miles, and changed the plans of the entire party for that night and for the rest of the trip.

I've been thinking, since that experience, that it's not only cars and carefree travelers, but also the work of whole institutions and the plans of communities and nations that are sometimes held up by tiny specks of dirt—for our purposes, false philosophies or untruths that thoughtless and sometimes scheming people place in our way.

(*Conference Report*, October, 1967, p. 123.)

PAUL H. DUNN

"Let's See If You Really Mean That"

An outstanding teacher was once listening to his wife play a beautiful sonata on the piano. "I would give anything in the world to be able to play like that," he said.

"All right," she responded. "Let's see if you really mean that. You say that you would give anything in the world to be able to play as I have. I have given several hours a day almost every day for the last fifteen years. I have given up picnics and parties and many other kinds of entertainment in order to stay at my task. I have sacrificed the study of many interesting subjects; I have given and worked and worked and given. At times it seemed that I could not work another hour or sacrifice another thing. To play the piano as well as I do, would you really be willing to give that much?"

(*Conference Report*, October 1968, p. 53.)

PAUL H. DUNN

"Not Ashamed to Be Identified"

Just recently we had the Minnesota Twins in Boston, playing a very exciting series; and as you know, we have on that ball club Brother Harmon Killebrew. Harmon Killebrew is not ashamed of the gospel of Jesus Christ. He is a quiet, silent, wonderful miracle worker. He called me on the phone one evening and said, "Paul, would it be possible in your schedule to come down Sunday morning and talk to the Minnesota Twins' ball club?" I said, "I'd be honored, Harmon, what can I do?" He said, "Just teach them the gospel of Jesus Christ, but don't tell them you are doing it." And I said, "Well, how did you get this program arranged?" And this great athlete said, "I'm the program chairman for our devotional services." I said, "I didn't know ball clubs had devotional services." He said, "The Minnesota Twins do, and I'm it." So I went down to the Statler-Hilton one Sunday morning, and there assembled before me were many Minnesota Twin ball players and their wives. That was exciting to me, and I am sure it would be to Coach Tuckett and a few others.

There in an upper room, in a quiet, peaceful, reverent manner, we talked, not all about baseball, although that entered a time or two, but about eternal verities that really change lives, goals and aspirations in their lives. . . . Harmon Killebrew is not ashamed to be identified.

(*Speeches of the Year,* "Be Not Ashamed," September 29, 1970, p. 3.)

PAUL H. DUNN

"Paul Dunn, Come Up Here"

I don't know whether I have shared this with you before, but you know sometimes little incidents in life can be great barriers later. I had one in the fifth grade. (I can remember back that far, I really can.) I was a student in the Little Rock, Arkansas, city schools. They were a little backward in some of their educational philosophies then, and this was in an era when you started in the first grade and you stayed with the same thirty students right through high school—they just promoted the class. Grades were secondary. So the peer group became quite a factor in my life—to be accepted, to be important, to be one of the gang.

I remember one incident that occurred in my English class. Down in Arkansas it gets pretty warm in the spring and the summer, real humid, and this was in the days before air-conditioning. (I was born even before TV, if you can imagine that!) I was sitting in this fifth-grade English class, dreaming about my mansions on high—do you ever do that, just day-dream?—and I was dreaming about one day being a great athlete. Right at that precise moment, my teacher called on me. She had a philosophy that when one's interest waned, call on him. Did you ever get a teacher like that?

117

This is the way she did it. She really snapped me back to reality. She said, "Paul Dunn, come up here!" I responded, and she handed me a piece of chalk as I walked up to the front of the class.

She said, "Young man, go to the board and diagram that sentence." (She had placed a sentence on the board.)

Well, I didn't know how you diagrammed a sentence, so I took the chalk and I walked to the board. Then I drew a big square around it, and I handed the chalk back to her.

She snatched it and she said, "I thought so. Come here, young man!" She stood me right in front of her desk and I was looking right into the eyes of my twenty-nine colleagues. There was a sweet little thing sitting on the second row, third seat, that I was trying to impress.

The teacher placed her hands very heavily on my shoulders, and said, "Class, I have been teaching English in this school, in this room, for over thirty years (I think that was part of her problem), and without a doubt, there is no question, this is the dumbest boy I've ever had!"

Now, you and I know that kind of comment doesn't build confidence. After hearing her expression of my abilities, I took a silent oath and covenant to never study again—not that I had done much up to that point anyway. And would you believe it, I actually didn't take a book home for the next seven years, and I've got report cards to prove it!

Well, isn't it sad sometimes what one misunderstanding person can do to our lives. I grew up for the next seven years thinking, "I'm a nothing. I'm a nobody. I can't."

Thank God for a father and a few great people who entered my life who said, "Oh, yes you can, when you find out who you really are."

(*Speeches of the Year*, "Know Thyself, Control Thyself, Give Thyself," October 7, 1969, pp. 8-9.)

PAUL H. DUNN

"I'll Race You to the Parking Lot"

Just last Thursday I had an opportunity to walk briefly to the temple with President McKay. I am happy to report to you that he is vigorous and active in the work, even though he is in his ninety-fourth year. I told him briefly that I would have a chance to come and share a few moments with you this morning, and this always brightens his day.

A few weeks ago I had the opportunity to take three young people about your age to see him in his hotel apartment. He and Sister McKay were occupying twin wheelchairs as we entered the living room. He chatted with each of these young people about their aspirations and goals and how they were preparing for life. It was a tender scene to be sure. Then as he took his seat again in the wheelchair—for he had insisted upon standing—we quietly excused ourselves. A member of his family had come in to announce that the car was ready in the garage to take them to Huntsville. This man who understands the gospel and its purposes has a tremendous zest for life. He leaned over and patted Emma Ray on the hand: "Come on, honey. I'll race you to the parking lot!"

(*Speeches of the Year*, "Keys to Successful Living," February 13, 1968, p. 3.)

PAUL H. DUNN

"Can You Qualify?"

One has said:

Two men look out
Through the self-same bars.
One sees the mud,
The other the stars.

It is a matter of point of view.

Opportunity is all about us. One of the processes that you are experiencing here at school is creating your own opportunities. Much could be said here. I think that, unfortunately, many Latter-day Saints tend to fall prey to the mediocre life —they have created little or no opportunity because they haven't fully capitalized on the talents and abilities they possess.

May I speak somewhat frankly. As an institute coordinator in Southern California I was privileged to be on some seventy different college campuses from time to time. It became quite well known that I was working with the college element— you. Thus, when both Latter-day Saint and nonmember business and industry leaders were looking for capable, dedicated people to hire, it was natural for them to call one who had daily contact with this trained element. No less than fifteen or twenty times a week I would receive telephone calls from some of the finest men of Southern California wanting to know about you.

I had in my desk almost continually job opportunities in more than fifty different categories. Do you know what my greatest problem was? I couldn't find Latter-day Saints qualified to fill them. Here is the paradox in our modern society —in any given week I would have five to ten college-age people walk into the office and say, in essence, "Brother Dunn, do you know where I can get a good job—a high-paying job?"

I would open up the drawer and bring out my list and say, "You bet. Can you qualify?" There was often the sad commentary: Here were young men with all the capacities and the ability in the world, but they hadn't taken the opportunity to develop them to their fullest. I suppose if anything pained my heart it was to see young men and young women terminate their education too soon because they lacked the vision to see what was ahead in the immediate future.

One illustration comes to mind. I have quoted it a time or two, but it is very fresh in that it occurred the week that I was called to assume this particular position.

The vice-president of the Purex Corporation in the Southern California region called me. (He is not a member of the Church.) As he identified himself, he said, "We have never met, Mr. Dunn, but I know a great deal about your program and your people, and I am so impressed with the philosophy and the point of view that your group represents, that I would like to fill six junior executive positions now available with your people. I will take any six that you send over to me, sight unseen, providing, number one, they have a bachelor's degree or its equivalent." We spelled out what he meant by "equivalent"—in terms of other experiences and exposure to educational programs.

Then I paused to ask him: "Do you want some specific area of concentration—liberal arts, engineering, mathematics orientation? What do you need?"

He said, "It doesn't matter. Industry today will specifically train the individual in these areas of detail. What we want is a person with a broad point of view, who has been exposed to the educational processes—one who can solve problems without asking for advice every few minutes."

The securing of an education, you see, teaches us how to think and to rationalize and to apply principles. And this is the same procedure used in businesses.

I said, "Fine. Thank you. What's the second point?" You would expect it, I am sure, knowing this particular group. He said, "That you recommend without reservation the moral character of the individual that you send. Is he honest, true, and virtuous? If he can pass those two tests, Mr. Dunn, he has the job."

Then he spelled out the job details. . . .

The sad part of this story is that from seventy college campuses, I could only get two of the positions filled. Within two to three weeks of this experience, however, I had no less than twenty-five returned missionaries come in who had *left school* seeking the opportunity of a lifetime. They were somewhat concerned as to why people would not take them on and give them all of the rewards of life. Isn't it interesting?

Industry indicates to all of us that at the top, in any field of endeavor, the vacancy sign is always posted.

(*Speeches of the Year*, "Three Basic Ingredients for Success," July 20, 1965, pp. 9-11.)

PAUL H. DUNN

"The New Testament Came Very Forcefully to My Mind"

The department of education provides, as you know, some very excellent Church facilities at the various colleges and universities. We have a number of such institute buildings in the southland. I have been using the Institute of Religion building at the University of Southern California for an office. This required that I travel frequently—in fact, daily—from my home in Downey to the USC campus and back.

I am the type of fellow who gets very concerned about being in a rut. I like a change of environment, new things, challenges. So quite frequently I will take a different road to work just to break the monotony. I hate driving there on the freeway, looking at all those license plates day after day.

One morning as I made a tour through the northern part of our fair city, I went down a street which I had not traveled before. Lo and behold! there was under construction one of the finest looking homes I had ever seen! This house struck my fancy because it was almost identical to a plan which my wife had hoped that we would one day build. Working for the Church, we realized it would not be possible, but we dreamed about it.

I found myself, more often than not, going that way just to see the progress of the home that was not even mine. I am sure you do things like this in your own way. A month or two had gone by; and as the house was about two-thirds completed, one morning as I passed that way I noticed that the workmen had ceased their labors. No work was being accomplished.

The days grew into weeks. The thing that gave me the most concern, as I am sure it did the owner, was that the once bright, shiny, new lumber was now starting to fade because it was not yet painted. It turned first to a light brown, a darker brown, and then to kind of an off-yellowish, indicating that the deterioration process had set in. I thought, as I made one of my frequent trips by that way, how unfortunate more insight and vision hadn't gone into the planning.

Then, one morning as I passed by to see if there had been any progress, one of the eternal truths of the New Testament came very forcefully to my mind as I viewed the situation. It is one I am sure you are familiar with. We all have read it many times in New Testament courses and studies. Luke records it this way. He tells about an incident in the life of the Savior when a great multitude gathered, and as they frequently did, commenced to ask questions in an attempt to trap him. In this particular setting the Savior makes a very profound observation, so profound that it is just as applicable here today as it was in the time in which he uttered it. He said, as he turned to meet the multitude.

For which of you, intending to build a tower, sitteth not down first, and counteth the cost, whether he have sufficient to finish it?

Lest haply, after he hath laid the foundation, and is not able to finish it, all that behold it begin to mock him,

Saying, This man began to build, and was not able to finish.

Then he goes on to suggest another possibility:

Or what king, going to make war against another king, sitteth not down first, and consulteth whether he be able with ten thousand to meet him that cometh against him with twenty thousand? (Luke 14:28-31.)

Now his logic here makes pretty good sense, doesn't it? We could make application to the tower the Savior refers to as it might apply to eternal life. We can say, in essence, "For which of us, intending to build eternal lives, sitteth not down first and consulteth whether we will have sufficient to complete the task?" The process of educating the body, the mind, and the spirit is the foundation on which this can be achieved.

(*Education Week Devotional,* "Blessed Are the Teachable," June 8, 1964, pp. 4-5.)

PAUL H. DUNN

"Elder, It Looks Like You've Been Through a Famine"

One of the great attributes of the Church is that we, too, are building men. I have under my direction in New England some 175 of the finest young men and women anywhere in the world. I have great faith and confidence in them and the things they do. We appreciate you fine parents who sacrifice so that your sons and daughters can fulfill missions. You are doing them a great service, and you in turn are being blessed. In private interview and in testimony meetings, they often express love for you and for their families. You may rest assured they are very happy.

I might just say here parenthetically that one of the challenges of a mission president is to keep a physical balance in missionaries as well as the spiritual and mental. I saw two of my assistants on my return home, and I noticed they had taken off about thirty pounds, which was needed. The Saints are good to them in the field. These same two assistants, in trying to help a little ninety-seven-pound weakling put on a little weight, on one occasion approached him and said, "Elder, it looks like you've been through a famine." And this sharp little elder came right back and said, "And you two look like you caused it."

(*Conference Report*, October 1970, p. 13.)

PAUL H. DUNN

"There Is Nothing I Don't Know"

My father-in-law, if you will permit another personal reference, was not a member of this Church. He was a great Protestant minister. I suppose if there was a counterpart of an apostle in the Disciple of Christ organization, this would have been his position. He was termed "minister-at-large," and he was called all over the world to represent this great body of individuals.

He was at one time the president of a university sponsored by their church, although it was much smaller than Brigham Young University. He later became the head of Brite Bible College at Texas Christian University, which would be their counterpart to BYU. In this position he frequently entertained, of course, correspondence from would-be faculty members.

Shortly after his death, as I was helping my wife and her good mother sort out some of his materials, I came across a very interesting letter which I would like very briefly to share with you. This was addressed to him by a member seeking a position on his faculty. It says:

My Dear Sir:

Notified May 21 that financial stress let me out here without disgrace because I was a latecomer on the faculty. I teach almost anything in modern French, German, and Spanish—language, literature, courses for teaching, scientific material, and phonetics. I have made thirty-one public addresses since last January 1st. I have taught in three high schools, one state teachers' college, two state universities, and three denominational colleges. War, pestilence, and famine—not inefficiency—make changes necessary.

Keep sane by hobby of music, by playing the flute, baritone bass, alto horns, clarinet, and cello. Can direct and lead choruses, bands, or orchestras, including the a cappella choir which is now so popular. Have taught the cello for years and can instruct in all band instruments. Keep well by physical education. Have long taught and can still instruct, as a side line, in corrective exercises, floor activities, and gymnasium, line apparatus, heavy German gymnastics, and swimming.

Health lecturer. Used repeatedly for institute work in this capacity. I prefer teaching to research, though I keep up advanced studies. Taught high school administration during seven summer sessions. Teacher of German this summer for the third time.

Your correspondence invited. Scholastic record enclosed.

Respectfully yours . . .

If you sat in the position of my father-in-law, making the decision as to whether you would include this man on your faculty, what would you do? If a like individual in your particular Church organization seemingly radiated this kind of egotism, would you be inclined to want to include him or her in the program? I do not mean to suggest, in running this fellow down, as it were, that we should not be self-confident in letting people know our ability and talents. But here is a man who suggests by his attitude that he has learned it all!

"There is nothing I don't know! You would be most fortunate to include me in your oganization." Chances are each of us would look very seriously for the individual who still had an attitude of wanting to learn more and one who would listen to the other fellow.

(*Education Week Devotional,* "Blessed Are The Teachable," June 8, 1964, pp. 6-7.)

PAUL H. DUNN

"Happiness Is Being Able to Walk"

I guess all of these things about happiness have caused me to be a bit on the alert, so the other day I was naturally interested when "Dear Abby" wrote about happiness. Do you get "Dear Abby" in the Provo papers? Maybe you have some of the other advice columns such as Ann Landers. Anyway, Abby had just received a letter from a young lady that defined her ideas concerning happiness. Let me share it with you. The letter comes, as they usually do, addressed to "Dear Abby." The girl says:

"Happiness is knowing your parents won't almost kill you if you come home a little late at night. Happiness is having your own bedroom. Happiness is having parents that trust you. Happiness is getting the phone call that you have been praying for all day. Happiness is getting good grades, and making your parents proud of you. Happiness is being included in the most popular circle. Happiness is in having parents who don't fight. Happiness is knowing that you are as well dressed as anyone else. Happiness is something I don't have. (Signed) Fifteen and Unhappy."

Abby was quite smart, I thought, on this occasion; rather than answering the letter directly, she invited the reading audience to submit their responses. May I share a few of their replies.

"Dear Fifteen and Unhappy: Happiness is coming home on time so your parents won't worry. Happiness is having someone to share a bedroom with. Happiness is proving to your parents that you can be trusted. Happiness is in realizing that sometimes you are lucky that you don't get what you pray for. Happiness is including someone who is lonely and unpopular in your circle. Happiness is having parents who stay together in spite of disagreements. Happiness is keeping the clothes you have neat and clean and not worrying about how they measure up to somebody else. Happiness is not something you get, it is is something you give. (signed) Fifteen and Happy."

Here is one from Vietnam.

"Dear Abby: We're a bunch of guys in Vietnam doing a job for Uncle Sam, and we read your column in *Stars and Stripes* the other day. That fifteen-year-old kid sure has a lot to learn, doesn't she? Do you know what happiness is for kids out here? Happiness is having enough to eat so that when you go to sleep at night your stomach doesn't ache. Happiness is having shoes on your feet and any kind of clothing to keep the cold out. Happiness is having a roof over your head. Happiness is being able to get any kind of an education some time in your life. Happiness is believing that the dream of freedom, brotherhood, and peace for mankind will someday come. (Signed) Some Very Happy GI's."

And then finally:

"Dear Abby: Happiness is being able to walk. Happiness is being able to talk. Happiness is being able to see. Happiness is being able to hear. Unhappiness is reading a letter from a fifteen-year-old girl who can do all of these things and still isn't happy. I can talk and I can see and I can hear, but I can't walk, but I am thirteen and real happy. (Signed) Thirteen and Happy."

(*Speeches of the Year*, "Happiness Is. . . ." April 18, 1967, p. 4-5.)

Paul H. Dunn

PAUL H. DUNN

"Builder of Men"

Fall also brings the crisp days and chilly nights that signal the start of the football season. Those of you who take an active interest in sports, and know of football's importance in turning boys into men, were saddened recently as I was in learning of the passing of that great football coach and builder of men, Vince Lombardi. Here was a man who came to a last-place team comprised of men who had forgotten what winning was—a team with no spirit, no confidence, and no respect—and in three short years he turned them into a team of world champions. But being a champion once didn't satisfy Vince Lombardi. He and his team went on to win again and again, game after game, title after title. The Green Bay Packers soon became the winningest team in professional football. Here was a man who could be as mean as a lion, yet gentle as a lamb. A man who said God and family should come first. A man who taught that not only physical toughness is important, but spiritual and mental toughness are also essential to success, and a man who said to all those who have problems and sometimes get discouraged, that "winning isn't everything, but wanting to win is."

I submit to you that we as a people, member and non-member alike, can learn some meaningful and timely lessons from the life of that great man.

(*Conference Report*, October 1970, pp. 12-13.)

PAUL H. DUNN

"Do You Have An American Flag?"

I had an opportunity, some years ago, to serve this great country as a World War II soldier. I am proud that I had the chance to serve. I love this country and what it represents. I would do it again and again. I am not here to argue the politics of whether we ought to be here or there at this time. I have my own convictions, but I have seen countries in serfdom. I know what slavery is. I know what a prison camp is. I know what happens when minds are directed to think only one thought. I had the opportunity, while on the Island of Guam as a PFC in World War II, to break down a concentration camp lock that had incarcerated many thousands of people for three years. I saw a Baptist minister in that camp, who although six feet tall weighed only seventy pounds, struggle through the mud to kiss my boot. He thanked me as an American liberator, because I represented a way of life that suggested great freedom. Do you know what his first request was? Tears in his eyes, lying there in the mud, he asked, "Soldier, do you have an American flag on you?" "No sir, I replied, "but I can get one." And I got one. And that man, so grateful for a new-found freedom, took that flag for what it was and what it represented and held it to his bosom and just cried. I know a little bit about such things because I was out there.

(*Speeches of the Year*, "Be Not Ashamed," September 29, 1970, p. 5.)

Biographical Sketch

Elder Alvin R. Dyer, an Assistant to the Council of the Twelve of The Church of Jesus Christ of Latter-day Saints, served in the First Presidency of the Church under the late President David O. McKay. He was ordained an apostle in October 1967 and served in the First Presidency from April 6, 1968, until President McKay's death January 18, 1970, at which time he resumed the calling as an Assistant to the Council of the Twelve.

While still president of the Central States Mission in April 1958 Elder Dyer was called to be the first assistant general superintendent of the Young Men's Mutual Improvement Association. After seven months he became an Assistant to the Council of the Twelve. He presided over the European Mission with headquarters in Frankfurt, Germany, from 1960 to 1962.

Elder Dyer, an engineer in the heating and ventilation field during his active business days, held membership in the American Society of Heating and Ventilating Engineers. During World War II he served as a member of the American Military Engineers, acting as a consultant. At one time he was active with the Exchange Club. During his service as president of the Central States Mission, he identified himself with the Missouri Historical Society, of which he is still a member.

Beyond high school, Elder Dyer obtained further education from many correspondence courses and other self teaching efforts. As a young man he became a journeyman sheet metal worker (1925-1933), which provided, with other things, a background for the heating and ventilating profession. He was manager of the heating and air conditioning department of the Utah Builders Supply from 1934 to 1949. He organized his own company, the Dyer Distributing Company, in 1949, which was highly successful. In 1956 he disposed of this company to devote all of his time to the Church.

One of thirteen children, Elder Dyer was born January 1, 1903 in Salt Lake City to Alfred Robert and Harriet Walsh Dyer. He married May Elizabeth Jackson in the Salt Lake Temple. They have two children, Gloria May Klein and Brent Rulon, and six grandchildren.

Elder Dyer has held many positions in the Church, extending back to 1924 when he returned from a twenty-six-month mission in the Eastern States, where he was the supervising elder of the New York District. He served as the superintendent of the Young Men's Mutual Improvement Association in the Sixteenth Ward of the Salt Lake Stake, after which he was called to be the first counselor in the bishopric of the Fifteenth Ward of the same stake, a position held for seven years. He subsequently served for eight years on two stake high councils, seven in the Salt Lake Stake and one in the Riverside. He later served as Sunday School superintendent of the Yalecrest Ward of the Bonneville Stake, and upon division of that ward he served as second counselor in the bishopric of the Monument Park Ward for three and one-half years and then as bishop for more than five years.

Elder Dyer is the author of many books, some dealing with history, such as *The Refiner's Fire* and *This Age of Confusion*. His many years of missionary service led to the publication of several books in this area. These are *The Challenge, The Meaning of Truth,* and *The Lord Speaketh*. Other books are *The*

Alvin R. Dyer

Fallacy and, most recent, *Who Am I?* The latter deals with the meaning of life and man's destiny.

Athletically minded, Elder Dyer played high school and semi-pro baseball and M Men basketball, and at one time bowled in major league circles. Of late he plays handball. At one time following his first mission, he had an opportunity to play professional baseball, but the offer was declined because of Church responsibilities.

ALVIN R. DYER

"Father Wants You To Come Back"

Here is a story that illustrates the response to a testimony borne from a sense of conviction. Two missionaries arrived at a home in the late afternoon. It was to be their last tracting visit for the day. It so happened that the family, with the father home, was just preparing to sit down to an early evening meal; they had planned as a family to go to the theater later. It was raining slightly as the missionaries began their door approach. Because of the anxiety of the mother at the door and the family for their evening plans, the missionaries had little success with their message at the door. However, not being aware of the situation in the home, the missionaries continued to declare their message, seeking the invitation to return and meet with the family in a cottage meeting. They could hear some voices from the inside of the house, one of which said, "Tell them to go away, the dinner is getting cold. We'll be late for the show." At this the woman began to close the door. Seizing the opportunity before it was too late, the missionaries ceased their door message and bore testimony to the truthfulness of the gospel and of the statements they had made. In bearing testimony, one of the elders purposely raised his voice so that those on the inside could hear it. In the meantime, the rain had increased and the missionaries left rather hurriedly from the doorstep as the door was closed.

They had half walked and run about half a block when they heard someone calling to them through the rain. They stopped to listen, and shortly a young man of about fourteen years of age caught up with them and said, "Father wants you to come back." So they returned to the home where an explanation was given to them as to the reason for their wanting to get on with the dinner and of their closing the door. The father said that he had not felt impressed with what he had heard at the door until the missionary bore his testimony. Then he said, "A strange feeling came over me, and I knew we had done wrong in sending you away." This awakened interest brought about by the testimony and the spirit of conviction led to the baptism of this family of five.

True conversion will serve as a compelling influence in our lives, leading to changes for the better. This motivating power of conviction produces a new and more righteous life. The individual who comes under its power is literally born again, as all must be to enter the kingdom of our Father. The Holy Ghost, then, will lead him unto truth.

(*Speeches of the Year,* "When Thou Art Converted," November 17, 1970, p. 4.)

ALVIN R. DYER

"Dr. Novinski"

I mentioned an experience, in talking to the married students some few weeks ago, of my visit to

Poland in the interest of laying the groundwork for the microfilming of the archives records of the Polish people, where even
now negotiations continue; and undoubtedly we shall have the
privilege of microfilming seventy-five million images which
include the birth, the marriage, and the death records of these
many people who lived anciently in this land, going back as
far as the fifteenth century. These will be added, in time, to
the vast genealogical research library of the Church from
which will come family group sheets and the relentless work of
going to the temple and doing vicariously for these ancient
people what they were unable to do for themselves because of
not having the gospel truths.[1]

It required a considerable amount of arrangement to get
into Poland. But because we were invited there by the government, many of these barriers were removed, making possible
the experience we had there in meeting with the archives officials of the Polish government in which this particular field
functions under the minister of education.

I recall at the conclusion of our discussions, when we had
done all that we could in making preparations for this, that we
desired to bear testimony of the truth of the gospel of Jesus
Christ, and the opportunity was provided for us when Dr.
Novinski, associated with the department of education, invited
me to tell them something about the Church. So there, in one
of the government buildings in Warsaw, we held a "share-the-
gospel" cottage meeting and had the opportunity, while speaking in German, a language which these people understood, to
bear testimony of the reality of the restoration of the gospel, of
the reason for the microfilming of genealogical records, of the
purpose of the Restored Church, and of its teachings and saving
ordinances. These men (and they had invited many of the
archives assistants to come in to this particular office) listened
almost spellbound. Our message was so different from anything
they had ever heard before. It seemed so distant to the conditions of living to which they were submitted and the beaten
paths that they had to follow under the unrighteous dominion
of their political situation. Finally, when the meeting was over,

---

[1]Actual microfilming is now in progress, 1971.

they asked us for literature. This is forbidden normally in that land, but these government officials *asked* for literature, which we gave to them in German.

We then had many hours before plane departure for Czechoslovakia, to which we had to fly enroute to Zurich to hold a stake conference in the Swiss Stake with Elder Howard W. Hunter. We were given the liberty of the city and permitted to take many pictures.

But there is one experience that came out of this that I want to mention this morning. As we traveled through the city we came to a certain area, and Dr. Novinski stopped the government car in the midst of a number of very wonderful buildings that had been recently constructed. These buildings were not ordinary structures. They were well built, indicating that the Polish people must have sacrificed other building needs to provide the materials for these, for there is a shortage of materials in Warsaw and in Poland. Dr. Novinski then explained that we were standing in the area once known as the Warsaw Ghetto—that infamous place to which the Jewish people of Europe were shipped from the conquered countries, there to await their eventual deportation to the exterminating chambers, which were not very far away.

As I stood there thinking of what the Polish people had done in erasing or endeavoring to erase from their memory the terrible experience of this place and the terrible inhumanities that had been brought upon the Jewish people, I thought of the experience of one of our young missionaries then serving in France who was in this ghetto with his mother and father. He is a Belgian Jew. When the time came for them to be taken to the gas chambers, he was with his parents at first, but somehow, in some way that he is not able to explain, from his written testimony to me, he was taken by the hand, by someone else and led out of the camp, thereby escaping the gas chamber. How this was accomplished he does not know, even now. At any rate he remained secreted in the environs of Warsaw and was not found.

(*Speeches of the Year*, "The Gospel of Jesus Christ Is Not Theory," May 9, 1962, pp. 4-5.)

"They Had No Permit"

We had another experience in leaving Poland to fly to Prague, Czechoslovakia, as Dr. Novinski bade farewell to us in the Drome (or the airport). We had grown attached to him and he to us. He said to Brother Arnold Seiler, who was my traveling companion, and myself, "You men are different. I have felt a spirit, and an influence, and a power that I have never experienced before." His eyes were blurred with tears as he spoke.

Of course this was not us. It was the Priesthood of God that we bore and carried with us into this land behind the Iron Curtain.

I felt and have seen the demonstration of this same power in meeting with the people in East Germany, where under regulation, under the strictest form of regulation, we carry on our Church program. The presidents of branches find it necessary each Monday to go to the police court and there obtain permits for the holding of meetings for that week. They can hold no other meetings in East Germany other than those for which they receive a permit. Upon one occasion, in the city of Dresden, one of our German sisters thought that she would have a few of the young people into her home in traditional Mormon fashion to have a fireside. She had prepared some nice things to serve, to try and keep from these young people the pressures and the influences that were crowding in upon them because of regulations behind the Iron Curtain. In the midst of their fireside the police came and demanded the showing of the permit for holding the meeting. They had no permit. They were fined 200 marks, which they had to pay, with a warning that if they held another that the fine would be much greater and the leaders might be sent to prison.

In Czechoslovakia we are not able to hold any meetings. The members of the Church continue within their hearts the love of the gospel and hope and dream for the day when they might be able to meet again and feel the association with their brothers and sisters.

In Poland we are permitted to meet, but we do not have many members there now—only about eighty-seven. They still meet, principally at Selbongen, but here also under extreme conditions.

(*Speeches of the Year*, "The Gospel of Jesus Christ Is Not Theory," May 9, 1962, p. 7.)

Biographical Sketch

PRESIDENT SPENCER W. KIMBALL

Spencer Woolley Kimball, Acting President of the Council of the Twelve of The Church of Jesus Christ of Latter-day Saints, is a public servant of long standing and varied experience.

He was born March 28, 1895. He was the sixth of eleven children born to his parents, Olive Woolley and Andrew Kimball. Andrew was one of the younger sons of Heber C. Kimball, apostle, prophet, missionary and counselor in the First Presidency of the Church. He was a member of the Council of the Twelve from 1835 to 1847, when he became a counselor to President Brigham Young until his death. Heber C. Kimball was one of the original twelve apostles of this dispensation.

Elder Kimball's maternal grandfather, Edwin Dilworth Woolley, was the business manager for President Brigham Young and was President Heber J. Grant's bishop.

Though born in Salt Lake City, he was destined to become an Arizonian, as his father was sent by the First Presidency of the Church to Thatcher in the rich Gila Valley to preside over the St. Joseph Stake, over which he presided for twenty-six and one half years, following a ten-year mission as president of the Indian Territory Mission.

Elder Kimball was first called on a mission to the Swiss-German Mission, but when the first world war began in 1914, he was transferred to the Central States Mission. During most of his twenty-eight months in the Central States Mission, he was president of the Missouri Conference. Since that early beginning in missionary work, he has visited missions and missionaries in all parts of the world, and now he is chairman of the executive committee of the missionary work for the Church in all the world, and has interviewed tens of thousands of missionaries.

Upon his return from his mission, he met Camilla Eyring, who was teaching in the Gila Junior College, and they were married in November, 1917. She was a refugee from Mexico, born in Colonia Juarez and, with her family, driven from that country in the time of the Villa Revolution.

Her education came from the Juarez Stake Academy, Brigham Young University, Utah State University and the University of California. She is the daughter of Edward Christian Eyring and Caroline Romney. They are the parents of four living children, three sons and one daughter, and they have twenty-seven grandchildren and six great-grandchildren as of 1971. He boasts of a family total of forty-five, and his family is central in his life. Their daughter, Mrs. Grant M. Mack (Olive Beth) is a member of the Tabernacle Choir. Spencer L. Kimball is dean of the University of Wisconsin, a Rhodes scholar, author of textbooks on insurance law, and former Dean of the University of Utah Law School. Andrew Kimball, of New York City, is prominent with General Electric. Edward is a professor of law at the University of Wisconsin.

Elder Kimball was called to be a member of the Council of the Twelve on July 8, 1943, and was ordained an apostle by President Heber J. Grant, October 7, 1943.

In his work on the Council of the Twelve, he has traveled the world around—to the Orient and to the Occident, in South America from the north to the south and Central America and Mexico many times; in Canada from east to west, in Europe in practically every country; in the South Pacific including the islands and New Zealand and Australia; and in the United

States from Maine to San Diego, and from Seattle to Florida, and in between. He has toured most missions, has visited most stakes, and has created many of the stakes, dividing and re-organizing in South America, the South Seas, Britain, America, and Canada. As a director he supervised missionary work in South America for three years and in Great Britain for two years, and now in his new work presides over all missions of the Church and is the chairman of the executive committee of the Missionary Committee for the Church.

Dating back to President Heber J. Grant's administration, Elder Kimball has been closely associated with and a leader in the Indian Program and was chairman of the Indian Committee for a quarter of a century. Under his leadership, much was done for the Indians, and he helped to institute the successful program now known as the Indian Student Placement Program and assisted in all the other development programs for the Indians.

He is the author of many pamphlets and one widely read book, *The Miracle of Forgiveness.*

SPENCER W. KIMBALL

"That First Tithing Receipt"

When I was a little boy in Thatcher, Arizona, my father, desiring to teach his children industry, thrift, and tithing, turned over to my sister Alice and me a patch of potatoes which he had planted.

I hoed the weeds and helped to irrigate the potatoes until they were ready to dig. Then Alice and I dug and cleaned and sorted them. We took the larger ones of uniform size and put them in a box and loaded them in my little red wagon. Then, after putting on clean overalls and dress, we pulled the little red wagon with its contents to town.

We sold our merchandise to some of the neighbors, but a kindly sister who operated the hotel was our best customer. She looked them over and bought from us regularly through the season.

After selling our first load we were so happy we could hardly wait to get home to tell our parents of our success.

Father listened to us count our money—a very great amount, it seemed to us. Then father inquired: "That's capital! Now what will you do with your money?"

We thought of ice cream cones and candy and Christmas

presents we could buy. Then in his characteristic and impressive way, our father said: "Now you haven't forgotten the bishop, have you? The Lord has been kind to us. The earth is his. He sent the moisture and the sunshine and all we did was to plow and plant and cultivate and harvest. One-tenth we always give back to the Lord for his work. When you have paid your tithing to the bishop, then you may use the balance as you wish."

I think I still have in my keepsakes that first tithing receipt.

(*Children's Friend*, April 1947, p. 147.)

SPENCER W. KIMBALL

"Still Smiling, in Her Wheel Chair"

In the recent past, I found honor and integrity in resplendent glory. I saw the trials of life multiply and culminate in a visit from the grim reaper. She was a young school teacher just reaching her majority. While decorating a Christmas tree, she had fallen from the ladder and broken her back and was consigned the rest of her life to a wheel chair. In her resourcefulness, she developed her memory through the years and became a reviewer of books, for which she received compensation to support herself. No vulgar books would she read or review. Time passed, and, from her wheel chair, she enthralled her numerous audiences. A book a month she absorbed, mastered, and made hers; and then she entertained her public. Years passed.

Illness came to her widowed sister who was bedridden. The wheel chair victim, from her captivity, waited upon the sister. And now her aging mother fell and broke her hip, and with two patients, this wheel chair nurse operated a miniature hospital. They both finally died and left her alone.

In the home, she carried on. Books and books—readings and readings. Her strong, clear voice was a call to courage. Her persistence in spite of many handicaps showed an indomitable will. No pity did she ask, nor succor, nor sympathy. She first read the book, wrote a condensation, then memorized the latter. Years passed. Her overworked vocal cords eventually became hoarse, and with it the means of her living was threatened. She used her precious voice as long as she could; then came the day when the hoarseness was diagnosed as treacherous cancer. Still smiling in her wheel chair, she asked nothing, finally giving up her reviews, then taking to her bed, with her voice petering out and her breath shortening; then to the hospital for short days of gasping; then to her grave. There was no blame, no bitterness, no moroseness, but smiles and thanks and gratitude. Facing sure death, she yet had no complaint, only sweetness and courage. *That is integrity.* Like Job of old, she knew that her Redeemer liveth.

(*Speeches of the Year,* "Integrity," February 25, 1964, pp. 7-8.)

SPENCER W. KIMBALL

*"Carry A Message to Garcia"**

The Rowan story is one well known to us all, but periodically every one should review *A Message to Garcia* by Elbert Hubbard:

*This story is not original with Elder Kimball.

In all this Cuban business, there is one man who stands out on the horizon of my memory like Mars at Perihelion.

When war broke out between Spain and the United States, it was very necessary to communicate quickly with the leader of the insurgents. GARCIA was somewhere in the fastnesses of Cuba—no one knew where. No mail or telegraph message could reach him. The President must secure his cooperation quickly.

WHAT TO DO!

Someone said to the President, "THERE IS A FELLOW BY THE NAME OF ROWAN WHO WILL FIND GARCIA FOR YOU IF ANYBODY CAN."

ROWAN was sent for and given a letter to be delivered to Garcia. How the "fellow by the name of Rowan" took the letter, sealed it up in an oilskin pouch, strapped it over his heart, in four days landed by night off the coast of Cuba from an open boat, disappeared into the jungle, and in three weeks came out on the other side of the island, having traversed a hostile country on foot, and delivered his letter to Garcia—are things I have no special desire now to tell in detail. The point that I wish to make is this: McKINLEY GAVE ROWAN A LETTER TO BE DELIVERED TO GARCIA: ROWAN TOOK THE LETTER AND DID NOT ASK: "Where is he at?" BY THE ETERNAL! THERE IS A MAN WHOSE FORM SHOULD BE CAST IN DEATHLESS BRONZE AND THE STATUE PLACED IN EVERY COLLEGE OF THE LAND. It is not the book learning young men need, or instruction about this or that, but a stiffening of the vertebrae which will cause them to be loyal to a trust, to act promptly, concentrate their energies: do the thing—CARRY A MESSAGE TO GARCIA.

GENERAL GARCIA IS NOW DEAD, but there are other Garcias. No man has endeavored to carry out an enterprise where many hands were needed but has been well-nigh appalled at times at the imbecility of the average man—the inability or unwillingness to concentrate on a thing and do it.

Slipshod assistance, foolish inattention, dowdy indifference, and half-hearted work seem the rule and no man succeeds, unless by hook, or crook, or threat he forces or bribes other men to assist him or mayhap, God in His goodness performs a miracle and sends him an Angel of Light for an assistant. . . .

(Speeches of the Year, "Integrity," February 25, 1964, pp. 14-15.)

SPENCER W. KIMBALL

"The Breaking of Day Has Found Me on My Knees"

My beloved brethren, this is the great day of my life. I have seen hands raised many times in my life, but never have they meant quite so much as they meant today when you raised your hands to sustain and support me.

I feel extremely humble in this calling that has come to me. Many people have asked me if I was surprised when it came. That, of course, is a very weak word for this experience. I was completely bewildered and shocked. I did have a premonition that this call was coming, but very brief, however. On the eighth of July, when President Clark called me I was electrified with a strong presentiment that something of this kind was going to happen. As I came home at noon, my boy was answering the telephone and he said, "Daddy, Salt Lake City is calling."

I had had many calls from Salt Lake City. They hadn't ever worried me like this one. I knew that I had no unfinished business in Salt Lake City, and the thought came over me

quickly, "You're going to be called to an important position."
Then I hurriedly swept it from my mind, because it seemed so
unworthy and so presumptuous, and I had convinced myself
that such a thing was impossible by the time that I heard President Clark's voice a thousand miles away saying: "Spencer, this
is Brother Clark speaking. The brethren have just called you
to fill one of the vacancies in the Quorum of the Twelve
Apostles."

Like a bolt of lightning it came. I did a great deal of
thinking in the brief moments that I was on the wire. There
were quite a number of things said about disposing of my business, moving to headquarters, and other things to be expected
of me. I couldn't repeat them all; my mind seemed to be traveling many paths all at once. I was dazed, almost numb with
the shock; a picture of my life spread out before me. It seemed
that I could see all of the people before me whom I had injured, or who had fancied that I had injured them, or to whom
I had given offense, and all the small petty things of my life.
I sensed immediately my inability and limitations and I cried
back, "Not me, Brother Clark! You can't mean that!" I was
virtually speechless. My heart pounded fiercely.

I recall two or three years ago, when Brother Lee was
giving his maiden address as an apostle of the Lord Jesus Christ
from this stand, as he told us of his experience through the night
after he had been notified of his call. I think I now know something about the experience he had. I have been going through
it for twelve weeks. I believe the brethren were very kind to
me in announcing my appointment when they did so that I might
make the necessary adjustments in my business affairs; but
perhaps they were more inspired to give me the time that I
needed for a long period of purification, for in those long days
and weeks I did a great deal of thinking and praying and fasting
and praying. There were conflicting thoughts that surged
through my mind—seeming voices saying: "You can't do the
work. You are not worthy. You have not the ability." And
always finally came the triumphant thought: "You must do the
work assigned; you must make yourself able, worthy, and
qualified." And the battle raged on.

I remember reading that Jacob wrestled all night, "until the breaking of the day," for a blessing; and I want to tell you that for eighty-five nights I have gone through that experience, wrestling for a blessing. Eighty-five times, the breaking of the day has found me on my knees praying to the Lord to help me and strengthen me and make me equal to this great responsibility that has come to me. I have not sought positions nor have I been ambitious. Promotions have continued to come faster than I felt I was prepared for them.

I remember when I was called to be a counselor in the stake presidency. I was in my twenties. President Grant came down to help to bury my father, who was the former stake president, and reorganize the stake. I was the stake clerk. I recall that some of my relatives came to President Grant, unknown to me, after I had been chosen and said, "President Grant, it's a mistake to call a young man like that to a position of responsibility and make an old man of him and tie him down." Finally, after some discussion, President Grant said very calmly, but firmly, "Well, Spencer has been called to this work, and he can do as he pleases about it." And of course when the call came, I accepted it gladly, and I have received great blessings therefrom.

(*Conference Report*, October 1943, pp. 15-16.)

SPENCER W. KIMBALL

"You Will See Him Someday as a Great Leader"

Just the other day one of my brethren came into the office to talk to me intimately and confidently. After closing the door, he said, "Spencer, your father was a prophet. He made a prediction that has literally come to pass, and I want to tell you about it." He continued. "Your father talked with me at the corral one evening. I had brought a load of pumpkins for his pigs. You were just a little boy and you were sitting there, milking the cows, and singing to them as you milked. Your father turned to me and said, 'Brother, that boy, Spencer, is an exceptional boy. He always tries to mind me, whatever I ask him to do. I have dedicated him to be one of the mouthpieces of the Lord—the Lord willing. You will see him some day as a great leader. I have dedicated him to the service of God, and he will become a mighty man in the Church.' "

I say this, not in the sense of boasting, but in humility and appreciation. It came to me as a great surprise when first I heard of it the other day. I knew my father was prophetic, and some day I hope to be able to tell you some of his many prophecies which have been literally fulfilled.

(*Conference Report*, October 1943, p. 17.)

SPENCER W. KIMBALL

"The Story of Lazarus"

Today I would like to talk to you about miraculous events, those happenings that are difficult of explanation and understanding. There are two kinds of miracles. There are temporal miracles and spiritual miracles. There are the miracles which affect the body, and those which affect the soul—the one somewhat temporary, the other much more permanent. Recently a young doctor came into my office, and it seemed from his general attitude that the greatest thing in all the world was his work of relieving pain and saving bodies and lives, protecting mortal lives. And I remembered a little incident in the book which many of you have read, *The Robe*, the story of Miriam, who in her very crippled condition kept herself hidden in her room. She became sour and bitter; nothing was good; she was very selfish. And then came along the Master in the story and touched her life. He didn't heal her body, but he touched her in such a way that her bitterness changed to sweetness, her selfishness to unselfishness. And each night when the sun was setting, her friends came and carried her out to the well in the center of the village where all the villagers came together. And there with her changed life she inspired the many who came to hear her beautiful voice as she sang from an understanding, a sweet, sympathetic heart.

Then I related to this young doctor the story of Lazarus, how he had been treated by the most skillful physician that has ever graced the earth, and how that physician emphasized the transcendency of the spiritual above the physical. Word was sent to the Saviour at considerable distance from Bethany, that his great friend Lazarus was very, very ill. But according to his own words he purposely delayed going to the death-bed scene two days, and then it took him a long time to get there. And he did it on purpose; he could have gone earlier and saved this man before he died. But this is what he said, "And I am glad for your sakes"—the sakes of the followers and the disciples that were with him—"And I glad for your sakes that I was not there, to the intent that ye may believe." It was better that this one man should die perhaps that these many might get a bit of the inspirational life of Jesus and his power, and might get an insight into the gospel that he was trying to teach to them. The sickness and death of Lazarus then provided this great opportunity for him to teach faith to a large number of people.

(*Assembly Addresses*, February 11, 1947, pp. 2-3.)

SPENCER W. KIMBALL

"Guests of the Lord"

Beloved students, you are guests here—guests of the Lord, whose funds pay in large measure for your education. You are guests of the Lord, his Church, his leaders, his administration, his people. You and your parents make a smaller but necessary contribution.

In a faraway land to the south is an old man, somewhat crippled, untrained. The children, several, are ragged; their clothes are hand-me-downs, and winter or summer they trudge barefooted to a little primitive school. The home is tiny—two small rooms, one under the other with a ladder connecting. The little mother makes baskets and sells at the public market. The father makes chairs and tables out of the native jungle trees and on his calloused, leathery bare feet, walks long distances, carrying his furniture those miles to market, hopefully. The middle man or the bargaining buyer leave him very little profit from his honest labor; but because he is a faithful member of the Church, he takes his tithing to his branch president. And it finally reaches the treasury house, and part of it allocated to the Brigham Young University. And he, this dear old man, and she, this deprived little mother, and they, these gaunt little children, along with their fellow members and numerous others who are tithepayers, become host to you—the guests—and supply a goodly percentage of the wherewithal for land and buildings and equipment and instructions.

The boy working in the cornfield in India is your host for he returns his ten percent.

The rich man living in his luxury who pays his tithing is your host.

The widowed mother with several hungry children is your hostess.

The janitor of your meeting house is your host.

The Navajo on the desert following his little band of sheep trying to find enough grass—he is your host. His dollars are few, his tithing is meager, but his testimony of the gospel, his dreams for his children, and his love for his fellowmen and his Lord induce him to send in his little tithing. He also becomes a joint host for you.

As guests we have opportunities and responsibilities. Our rights are few. Our demands should be fewer. As guests we gratefully accept the favors of our hosts and hostesses.

Would a guest attend a banquet uninvited? Would he dress in fatigue clothes when the host had set it up as a "black tie" affair? Would he respect the host and his position? Would he say disparaging things about his host even while accepting of his hospitality? Would he declare his freedom to eat with his fingers, laugh raucously, tell malignant stories about his host?

Would he come early or stay too late? Would he take with him the host's treasures? Would he monopolize the conversation and disregard the wishes of the host? Would he ill-behave himself, ignore the wishes of the host, or defy his requests?

Would he march or riot or demand? Would he criticize— the house too small, the temperature not right, the cook ugly, the waitresses inefficient? Because other guests have been known to be unruly, would he take license therefrom? Because other guests at other houses of hospitality destroy the property of their host, lock the doors, sit in or sleep in, would these guests follow suit?

Would guests come ill-clad? uncut? unbathed? unwashed? Would a guest belittle his host or embarrass him? Would guests declare their independence, forget their opportunities or demand their supposed rights?

The greatest of all universities is our joint blessing. Let us all together keep it the pleasant oasis in the desert, where there is water and coolness when the desert sands blast in their fury.

Let us keep it an island of beauty and cleanness in an ocean of filth and destruction and disease. Let us keep it as a spring of pure cool water though surrounded by sloughs and stagnant swamps of rebellion and corruption and worldliness outside.

Let us keep it a place of peace in a world of confusion, frustration, mental abberations, and emotional disturbances. Let us keep it a place of safety in a world of violence where laws are ignored, criminals coddled, enforcement curtailed, buildings burned, stores looted, lives endangered.

May we keep this glorious place a home of friendships and of eternal commitments; a place of study and growth and improvement; a place where ambition is kindled and faith is nurtured and confidence strengthened, and where love for God and our fellowmen reaches its highest fulfillment.

Let it continue to be a place of confidence and common admiration and understanding, with students and instructors and staff all people of confidence, affection, and serenity.

Let us not regard this as just another university—not just classrooms and professors, and students and books and laboratories.

May we enjoy the privileges and opportunities of this great institution, and profit by our rich experience here, and extend our continued gratitude to the Lord and the joint hosts and hostesses in their gracious and generous hospitality.

My beloved young folks, stand by your guns. Stay true. Live the gospel. Love the Lord, I beg of you, in the name of Jesus Christ. Amen.

(*Speeches of the Year*, "In the World But Not of It," May 14, 1968, pp. 12-14.)

Biographical Sketch

ELDER MARK E. PETERSEN

Mark E. Petersen has spent his entire life working with words—spoken words and written words, but always words. Words in his hands come alive. They seem to mean more, to carry greater urgency, to more clearly unravel a theme than they might otherwise do.

Merely listening to or reading Mark E. Petersen's words seems to tell one what manner of man is he. His forceful baritone voice, controlled by flawlessly distinct diction, betrays an original eloquence and tremendous energy.

Much of what Mark E. Petersen is reflects his early journalistic career. He was born with a twin sister November 7, 1900, in Salt Lake City to humble Danish converts, Christian and Christine Anderson Petersen. As a young boy Mark became a news carrier in order to help earn his own way at home. On Saturdays and during summers he helped in his father's small construction business. A love for work with wood was instilled that still remains today.

Following his mission to Nova Scotia, twenty-three-year-old Mark joined the *Deseret News* as cub reporter.

Mark Petersen's innate abilities and honest character

flourished in such an environment, and within a few years his leadership capacity had led him through positions of news editor, managing editor, editor, general manager and president of Deseret News Publishing Company. He is also chairman of its board of directors and a director of the Newspaper Agency Corporation.

The year before Mark Petersen began his newspaper career he married Emma Marr McDonald. They have two daughters.

A few years later, Elder Petersen was asked to serve on the Sunday School general board. By the time he was managing editor he had also served on two high councils, had been second counselor in one stake presidency and first counselor in another, and had toured much of the Church, conducting conventions as a director of the Genealogical Society.

In 1944, at the age of forty-three, he was called to the apostleship and entered a new career, that of witnessing to all the world the truth about Jesus Christ. Elder Petersen presently supervises missions of the Church in the eastern United States.

His training with words is now sowing its seeds. He has authored innumerable pamphlets, tracts, booklets, books and Church editorials and is an unusually gifted speaker.

His daily training of handling major problems—particularly at getting to the heart of a problem—now finds lifetime use in the service of the Lord.

MARK E. PETERSEN

"I Was Blind"

Not very long ago I was down in one of the California stakes attending a stake conference. At the close of the morning meeting, one of the bishops brought his mother to the stand, as she wished to shake hands and send a message back home. When she reached the stand, she said, "Will you give a message from me to Brother Thomas E. McKay?"*

I said, "I shall be very glad to."

She said: "It has been a couple of years since he was here to stake conference, but I want you to take a message to him."

At that time I was holding in my hands a Book of Mormon that I had used during the conference. She took the Book of Mormon from my hands and opened it and read a paragraph to me; then she closed the book and gave it back.

She said, "Two years ago Elder Thomas E. McKay was down here to our stake conference. I was blind. I knew that if he would lay his hands upon my head I would receive my sight again. I sent over to the conference and had him come. He and the other brethren laid their hands upon my head

---

*An Assistant to the Council of the Twelve and President David O. McKay's brother.

and blessed me. Now you see that without even the use of glasses I have been able to read a paragraph from your book. When you get back to Salt Lake City, will you tell him what I have done here today and express to him the gratitude I feel to the Lord that one of his chosen servants came down here and was willing to lay his hands upon my head. Whereas I was blind two years ago, now I can see and I can read without glasses."

I thought that was a beautiful testimony she bore to one of the servants of God. I have loved Brother McKay ever since I first became acquainted with him some years ago.

(*Conference Report*, October 1951, p. 20.)

MARK E. PETERSEN

"A Friend of Mine Whom I Shall Call Bill"

I would like to tell you a story about a friend of mine whom I shall call Bill, for the sake of anonymity. During Bill's last year at school, he met a lovely young woman named Helen. They became very good friends, and it wasn't very long until they began to talk about the possibility of their getting married.

During that same last year of school Bill fell in with a group of fellows who were known as the most popular group on the campus. They taught Bill some bad habits.

When Helen first saw Bill with a cigarette in his mouth, it nearly broke her heart. She talked with him and pleaded with him, but he felt that smoking cigarettes was one of the things that went with the popularity of this group on the campus. So her pleadings brought no results. Helen began to wonder if she should stay with Bill or not, whether she should allow their courtship to end in marriage. She wanted to be married in the temple, and she knew that if Bill continued to smoke cigarettes they would not get to the temple.

When graduation time came, Bill offered a formal proposal to Helen and asked her to set the date of their wedding. She thought it over long and seriously. She loved Bill a very great deal and did not like the idea of losing him. But neither did she like the idea of marrying a smoking man, one who could not take her into the temple where she had wanted to go.

After some days' consideration, Helen finally came to the conclusion that when school was out, Bill would be separated from this group of boys and that possibly, if she married him, under her influence he might leave off the bad habits which he had acquired and get back into activity in the Church. And then, probably within a year or so, they could go to the temple together; so she consented, and they were married by her bishop in her living room at home.

A year or so went by, and a lovely baby boy was born to them. They called him John. In due time another boy was born to them. They called him James, but he was soon known as Jim.

Bill loved his two boys, and every night after he came home from work, he would play with them and have just a grand time. He would hold them way above his head and laugh at them and talk to them, and they would laugh back. Then he would bring them down and hug them to him.

This show of affection made Helen very happy, but Bill played with them while he had a cigarette in his mouth, and when Helen saw those little baby hands reach out for that smoldering white thing between Bill's lips, her heart sank, and she began to wonder what that example might mean in the future lives of those boys.

Years went by. John became twenty years of age and was called on a mission. He was thrilled with the call and so was his mother. Bill—well, on the night of the farewell testimonial, Bill sat on the stand with his wife and son and he was just about as proud as any father could be, because John was really a remarkably fine young man.

About three weeks after John's departure for his mission, Bill was sitting one evening in front of the big, open fireplace in the living room reading the evening paper and smoking a cigarette. While he was doing so, in came Jim, a young man by this time. Jim said, "Hi Dad."

Without looking up from his paper, Bill said, "Hello, Son. How are you?"

"I'm fine, Dad. I want to ask you a question."

"All right, Son, what is it?"

"What's the best brand of cigarettes?"

Bill stiffened in his chair. For a moment it seemed as if he were frozen there. Then his hands relaxed, and the paper slipped from his fingers and fell to the floor. He flipped his cigarette over into the open fire and then stood up and faced his son.

He said, "Jim, you cannot start to smoke."

"But I have started already, and I want to know what is the best brand of cigarettes?"

"Son, I am telling you," Bill said, "you cannot start to smoke."

"Well, why not, Dad? You've smoked as long as I can remember, and it hasn't hurt you any. I've watched you."

Those last words Jim spoke cut into Bill's heart. "I've watched you. I've watched you." Then Helen was right, Bill thought to himself. All these years Helen had told him that his cigarette habit—the example he was holding before his sons—would result like this, and he had never believed her. Now Helen was right. Here was Jim saying, "I've watched you. I've watched you."

Then Bill felt a consciousness of guilt, a note of self-accusation, and there were words going through his mind saying, "I taught him, I taught him, I taught him."

Bill shook himself and walked over to his son and took hold of both shoulders and looked him square in the eye and said, "Son, you say these cigarettes didn't ever hurt me. And you say you've watched me. I want you to know that these cigarettes have done me more harm than anything else in my life. Nothing has hurt me, nothing has handicapped me so much as these cigarettes. Why, I'd give anything that I own if I had never started to use them, and I don't want to see the same handicaps come to you. Why, Jim, these cigarettes have raised a barrier between me and happiness right here in my own home, and they have caused your mother many hours of weeping. I know that, and I don't want you to undertake a habit of this kind."

He talked so earnestly and so unusually that Jim at first thought that his Dad was putting on an act and told him so. Again Bill began to talk and plead with his son never to smoke again, to get rid of this habit that he had just begun.

Then Jim, realizing that his dad was really serious, said, "Well, Dad, if this cigarette habit is so bad, why haven't you quit?"

Bill said, "I've tried to quit. I've tried many times, but I have never been able to—the habit is too strong. I'm just like a slave to the cigarette, and I don't want you to become a slave. Now, Son, cut it out."

Jim said, "Well, Dad, you see all the fellows I go with— they all smoke. They'll think I'm a sissy. I couldn't face those fellows and tell them I wasn't going to smoke any more. They are the most popular crowd I know."

Bill said, "Popular or not, stop this habit and if necessary get a new crowd. Find new friends who don't smoke, but let cigarettes alone."

Jim said, "Well, I don't know whether I can do that or not. I'll have to think this over."

Then his dad said, "Jim, I'll make a bargain with you. If you'll quit smoking, I'll quit."

Jim, quick as a flash said, "Well, Dad, you just told me you couldn't quit. Are you trying to lead me along?"

Bill's answer to that was that he walked over to the fire-place, put his hand in his pocket, pulled out the package of cigarettes and the folder of matches, and threw them into the open fireplace. Then he turned around and faced his son and said, "Son, I've quit. I'm all through. Now, will you do the same thing?"

"Well I don't know, Dad; I've got to think this over," Jim said, "I'll tell you in the morning."

That night Bill couldn't sleep. He rolled and tossed in bed as long as he could stand it and then got up and went into the living room and closed the door. He didn't turn on the lights. He just walked the floor there in the dark. Jim's words kept going through his head, "I've watched you. I've watched you," followed by his own sense of self-accusation, "I taught him. I taught him."

It had been a long time since Bill had said a prayer. He had left that pretty much with Helen. But this night he wanted more than anything else to have Jim quit smoking; so there in the darkness and the stillness of his home he slipped down on his knees and began to pray. He poured out his soul to the Lord and told him all of his faults and shortcomings, confessed all of his sins to the Lord—the first time he'd ever done that. Then he told the Lord about Jim and their conversation of the evening.

He didn't pray with much faith. The cigarettes had pretty well weakened what faith he had, but he did pray from a sense of fear—fear for the future of that boy—and from a sense of love—love for a son for whom he would give his own life, if necessary. But it seemed like asking a great deal of the Lord to erase in one night an example which he had held before his son ever since that son was a tiny baby.

At last morning came. Bill slowly climbed the stairs up to Jim's room and went in and sat down on the edge of the bed. He put one hand on Jim's shoulder. Jim turned over, and Bill said, "Son, what's your answer?"

Jim looked up into his dad's tired face and sleepless eyes and said, "Dad, I surely don't want to hurt your feelings, but the fellows—I couldn't face them. I guess I won't quit. I'll wait awhile."

Deeply disappointed, but without saying another word, Bill got up and walked slowly out of the room. He felt like he had been whipped. But he was more than ever determined to keep his own resolution. He would never go back to his cigarettes.

The next Sunday he went to church, the first time in years. He went again the next Sunday and the next, and he continued to go and enjoyed it.

About a year afterwards the bishop came to him one day and said, "Bill, how would you like to be ordained an elder?"

A lump came into Bill's throat, and his eyes filled with tears as he took hold of the bishop's hand and said, "Bishop, do you mean that at last I can take Helen to the temple?"

The bishop squeezed his hand and said, "Yes, Bill, at last you can take Helen to the temple."

Another year went by, and John came home from his mission. One day when John and his father were alone together, John went over and put his arm around his dad and said, "Dad, I want you to know how deeply grateful I am to you for the wonderful thing you have done. You know, as a boy I always used to think that my dad was just about perfect, and I guess every boy thinks that his dad is the greatest man in the world. But every time you took a cigarette, it hurt me deep inside. I knew you had a weakness you couldn't control. But now, Dad, all that is over, and I want you to know how grateful I am to you."

But what about Jim? Well, Jim is married now and has a little boy of his own, and he comes home at night and plays with his boy just as Bill used to play with Jim. And when Jim gets his own little son up in his arms, that little baby, just as his father did, reaches out for that smoldering white thing between his dad's lips.

The other day I rode home on the bus with Bill, and he was telling me how happy he is in his new life. And then he told me about Jim, and said that if nearly twenty years of bad example would put Jim where he now is, possibly another twenty years of a good example might bring him back to where he ought to be. And I thought, "God bless you, Bill."

And God bless all other men like him in the wonderful struggle they are making for the right.

And God bless Jim and all other boys like him that they

may recognize tobacco for what it is—a narcotic which enslaves human beings and helps to destroy their faith in God. This is my prayer, in Jesus' name. Amen.

(*Conference Report*, September 1950, pp. 38-42.)

M A R K   E .   P E T E R S E N

"Dare to Be a Mormon"

Last June I had the privilege of standing here and talking with the young people who came to the MIA conference. I told them about a little family up in Canada which had joined the Church, and as a result had suffered great persecution. To bolster their courage, this little family rewrote the words to a hymn they used to sing and made one of the verses go like this:

> Dare to be a Mormon;
> Dare to stand alone;
> Dare to have a purpose firm;
> Dare to make it known!

I invited the young people who were here last June to develop the same kind of courage held by this wonderful Canadian family, and in the face of all forms of opposition to stand firm and true to the faith.

That opposition might come in various forms. It might be persecution, as in the case of that Canadian family. It might be temptations, or it might come in the form of teachings from people who would like to destroy your faith.

When those temptations or those persecutions or those

false teachings come, will you have the courage to be real
Latter-day Saints, to have a purpose firm, and to stand by it?

(*Conference, Report* April 1952, p. 104.)

MARK E. PETERSEN

"Who Is Responsible?"

I remember so well a good sister
coming to my office one day. She sat at my desk in tears and
kept saying over and over to herself, "Why should this happen
to me? Why should this happen to me? Why should this happen to me?" When she was able to compose herself, she told
me about her boy who was in jail, having committed a serious
crime. And she said again, "Why should this ever happen to
me?" The boy had committed his crime under the influence of
alcohol.

When I found out more about this family, I learned that
this was the case: The father and mother used to argue a
good deal over the breakfast table. The mother loved her cup
of coffee. She simply had to have her cup of coffee. The father
always talked with mother about it, asked her to live the
Word of Wisdom, asked her to drink something else for breakfast. And always mother would say, "You can't tell me that a
cup of coffee will ever keep me out of heaven. You can't tell
me that the Lord is going to be so narrowminded that he will
keep me out of heaven when I go to church regularly, just because I drink a cup of coffee." Always she justified herself in
breaking that part of the Word of Wisdom.

There was, sitting at that breakfast table, a little boy. That little boy listened to the conversation between father and mother, and as the mother defended her infraction of the Word of Wisdom, as the mother said that the cup of coffee would not matter and the Word of Wisdom really did not matter either, that little boy believed his mother.

When he got a little older, he still believed his mother. When he started going with boys who smoked, he began to smoke. His mother had taught him that the Word of Wisdom really did not matter. "If it did not matter to Mother, if it would not stand in the way of her salvation, why should it matter to me? How can it keep me out of heaven, if it does not keep Mother out of heaven?" he would say to himself as he also justified his actions.

And so as the mother taught him to break the Word of Wisdom, he took up the habit of smoking. When he went to college and joined a certain fraternity where drinking was the custom, he began to drink. One night under the influence of liquor he committed a serious crime and went to jail. And now the mother sat at my desk, weeping and saying, "Why should this ever happen to me?"

There is another couple. They also talk over the breakfast table and over the dinner table, and by their conversation they also teach their children certain things. Mother and father see eye to eye in this family. They agree perfectly, and they talk over the things on which they agree as they sit there at dinner or breakfast. And do you know what the principal topic of conversation is? The bishop. How they despise the bishop! How they could tear him limb from limb! Everything the bishop does is wrong. Why nothing in the world that bishop does could possibly be right. That father and mother sit there picking at the bishop and pulling him apart, and depreciating him, and doing all they can to make each other feel that the bishop is a most unworthy representative of the Church.

Did it hurt the bishop? The bishop went right on doing a fine job in the ward. But somebody was hurt. There was a little boy in that family, also. Whom did he believe? He believed father and mother. He had no reason to disbelieve them.

They were his ideals. They were the law in that family. And when they, who laid down the law, constantly taught that boy by their own conversation to have no regard for the bishop, no regard for anything that the bishop did, they taught the boy to disregard everything for which a bishop stands.

That boy is now a grown young man. He does nothing in the Church. He has no respect for the Church, no respect for his bishop, nor for the men who installed the bishop.

Who is responsible?

(*Conference Report*, October 1952, pp. 29-30.)

MARK E. PETERSEN

"On My Honor"

On a recent trip I was a guest in the home of a little boy about six or seven years of age. He was looking through his older brother's Boy Scout handbook. He had turned to the section on tracking, where Scouts are taught to follow footprints of animals. He told me that he expects that this coming summer he will be out tracking, following footprints.

I looked beyond the footprints of animals to the footprints of human beings, and wondered whose foot tracks he would follow as he grew up. I wondered if they would be good tracks or bad tracks, and if the people who would make those tracks would be uplifting or degrading in their influence on him.

I picked up his book and turned to the section where I

read the Boy Scout oath. You remember the first few words are, "On my honor I will do my best. . . ." As he grows up, what will this little boy learn about honor or dishonor? Who will teach him? Or does it really matter? How important is honor, anyway? Is it something sacred? Is it sacred to you? Is it sacred to very many Americans?

In my opinion, America needs a rebirth of honor more than it needs any other one thing. . . .

My mind goes back to the little boy with the Scout manual. What if every American could but learn the first great lesson in that manual, the lesson of honor? What if every man were as honorable as he expects his son to be? What if every woman were as honorable as she hopes her children will be? What if every boy and girl had honor enthroned in their hearts and could pledge to all men that on that sacred honor they would do their best in life?

There is no happiness without honor. There is little success without doing one's best.

(*Conference Report*, April 1960, pp. 37-38.)

Biographical Sketch

PRESIDENT HARTMAN RECTOR, JR.

Elder Hartman Rector, Jr., a member of the First Council of Seventy of The Church of Jesus Christ of Latter-day Saints since April, 1968, served as supervisor of the European-Germanic and Italian missions of the Church. He now presides over the Alabama-Florida Mission of the Church, with headquarters in Tallahassee, Florida.

A former naval aviator, he holds the rank of captain in the United States Naval Reserve, and for ten years was with the U.S. Department of Agriculture where he was program and budget analyst in the office of Budget and Finance in Washington, D.C.

Elder Rector is a convert to the Church, having been converted in 1952 along with his wife, Constance Kirk Daniel, whom he married in 1947. They are the parents of seven children.

Elder Rector was born August 20, 1924, at Moberly, Missouri, a son of Hartman and Vivian Fay Garvin Rector. He was reared on a farm near Moberly, where he graduated from high school and junior college. In 1942, he enlisted in the Naval Reserve aviation cadet program, became a naval aviator, and was commissioned in 1945 with the rank of ensign. He was released from active duty in 1947, but was recalled in 1951 and saw action in Korea, remaining on active duty until April, 1958.

During his service in the Navy he received additional education at several colleges and universities, including Murray State Teachers College in Kentucky and the University of Southern California in Los Angeles.

He was ordained an elder in 1952 and a seventy in May, 1956. He has served the Church in many positions, including four and one-half years as a stake missionary. He was a counselor for one year in the Washington Stake mission presidency and for two years was stake mission president. He was a president in the 253rd Quorum of Seventy for three years, was stake MIA superintendent for three years, and for five years was the senior president of the 542nd Quorum. He also served five years as a ward seminary teacher.

Mrs. Rector has also served in many Church positions, including ward Primary and YWMIA president and member of the Potomac Stake Relief Society presidency.

HARTMAN RECTOR, JR.

*"Radio Tubes"**

Some time ago I heard a story told by President Harold B. Lee that I think very vividly depicts the condition which we must achieve. Brother Lee was serving as a stake president at the time he had this experience. He had a very serious and difficult case come before him wherein a man was accused of adultery but refused to admit that he had committed the act. However, he was tried for his membership, and the court found him guilty. He was excommunicated. Shortly thereafter this man's brother came to President Lee and said, "I have prayed to the Lord and I know that my brother is innocent. And so you have excommunicated an innocent man." President Lee said, "Brother, could we talk about this a little bit. I wonder if you would mind answering a few questions for me?" He said he would be willing to answer any questions.

Brother Lee proceeded to conduct an interview with him. He asked, "Do you drink coffee?"

And this brother said, "Yes, I drink coffee."

He asked, "Do you smoke?"

---

*President Rector related this story essentially as President Lee told it; however, every detail may not be totally accurate.

The man replied, "Yes, when someone gives me a cigar, I'll smoke a cigar."

"You drink tea?"

"Yes, iced tea."

"Drink alcohol?"

"Well," he said, "I have been known to take a drink."

"Do you fast?"

He answered, "No, my health won't allow it."

"Do you read the scriptures?"

He said, "No, I have problems reading the scriptures because my eyes are bad."

"Do you pay tithing?"

"No, and I am not going to pay tithing as long as that man is bishop of my ward."

"Do you hold family prayer?"

"No, our time is a little bit tight. We don't have time for family prayer."

President Lee said, "Well, brother, I have a beautiful instrument sitting in my home. It is called a radio. It is full of electronic devices called tubes, and when those tubes are strong and good, I can pick up a signal from the other side of the world and separate those signals. I can hear the voice clearly from halfway around the world. But," he said, "when those tubes become a little weak, when they begin not to function properly, then I have trouble separating the signal; I get a lot of static. There is one tube in that set called a rectifier. When the tube goes out, the set is dead. It then receives no signals at all. Now," he said, "in each one of us there are also some tubes. There is the Word of Wisdom Tube, there is the tithing tube, there is a scripture tube. When any of these tubes becomes weak, the signals get garbled. There is also a master tube in every one of us called the moral cleanliness tube. When that tube goes out, we have total darkness. There were fifteen men in this stake, last evening, who had fasted and prayed unto the Lord. They live the commandments as well as any fifteen men in this stake. They were unanimous in their decision that your brother was guilty. Now, you, who are living none of these commandments by your own admission, say you got a different answer when you prayed to the Lord. Whom do you suppose you may have been listening to?" And this brother said, "Well, I might have gotten my information from the wrong source."

(*Speeches of the Year*, "Get Up and Glow," January 5, 1971, pp. 4-5.)

H A R T M A N   R E C T O R ,   J R .

"Your Decisions Will Make You"

Now sometimes there are problems that you face that really aren't significant enough for the Lord to bother with. You think, "Well, I don't understand that. The Lord is supposed to answer all my prayers."

There is some good evidence in Section 61 of the Doctrine and Covenants that illustrates what I am talking about. This is where the Prophet and his party were traveling between Independence and St. Louis, Missouri, on the Missouri River. They had been given direction that a number of the party should go quickly on a mission. And as they were riding down the Missouri River one of the brethren saw, in open vision, the devil riding on the face of the water. That so startled them all that they stopped. They pulled over to shore in their boat and decided they had better talk this over. They talked about it among themselves, and they were in disagreement. One said, "Oh, the water is cursed, so let's don't go on the water, let's go on land."

Others said, "No, we are doing the work of the Lord, therefore he is going to protect us. It will be just as safe on the water as it will be on the land."

183

They couldn't agree and so they didn't do anything. They just sat there. They sat there all night. The next morning the Prophet prayed to the Lord and received an answer. It is a very interesting answer, part of which reads as follows:

"I, the Lord, was angry with you yesterday, but today mine anger is turned away.

"Wherefore, let those concerning whom I have spoken, that should take their journey in haste—again I say unto you, let them take their journey in haste.

"And it mattereth not unto me, after a little, if it so be that they fill their mission, whether they go by water or by land; . . . (D&C 61:20-22.)

In other words, "It doesn't make any difference to me how you go, but get going. Move out." And so it is important that you make a decision on your own sometimes.

I had a friend with whom I worked very closely as a counselor, who would sometimes come to me for decisions because that is what a counselor is for, to give counsel. It didn't mean he had to take my counsel, you understand. Many times he didn't and things prospered very well.

But he wanted guidance on the very smallest decisions; for example, should we hold our fast and testimony meeting at 9:00 or should we hold it at 9:15.

And I would say, "Well, 9:00 sounds all right to me."

He said, "Why do you say 9:00?"

I said, "Well, that's a good round number and everybody will be up by then and I don't really think it makes a whole lot of difference, so why don't you just have it at 9:00."

"But what about 9:15?"

I said, "Well, since you mention it, 9:15 may be better. You know how the Saints are at arriving at meetings on time. At least we'll have them all there by 9:15, so let's have it at 9:15."

And he said, "Do you really like 9:15?"

I said, "Well, I'm sure that the Spirit will be there by then, since we will have most of the people there."

He said, "You like 9:15. What about 9:00?"

So back and forth we would go, and finally I would say,

"I don't think it makes any difference: 9:00 or 9:15, either one will be fine."

Sometimes we belabor the Lord on little insignificant things like this on which we are perfectly capable of making the decision. It really won't make any difference to him. He told them here he didn't care whether they went by water or by land—just go. Be sure and get the job done—but go.

If you live for it, you deserve and can have the guidance of the Spirit in making decisions. And that, of course, is the thing that is most important, because the Lord knows the end from the beginning; things that sometimes appear insignificant to you on the surface may not be. If you are in tune, the Spirit will tell you, for instance, whether or not you should accept a call to fill a stake mission when you had planned on going to night school—it may seem insignificant. A lot of such calls are turned down, yet this may be a very significant decision in your life because it could put you on a course that will lead you to exaltation.

The Lord knows why you are here. Many times you don't know. Consider the course we have talked about today, think about it, weigh, seek advice of people who have been through the experience, pray unto the Lord, be clear on your principles and don't depart from them, and then all those decisions that deal with honesty and virtue and other things of eternal import will be made for you in advance. Take advantage of your advance preparation. That is the easy way to do it. Keep yourself in condition so you can get the spirit of the Lord, the guidance of the Spirit in all that you do. Then your decisions will be good decisions. Your decisions will *make you* . . . .

(*Speeches of the Year,* "Decisions Make Us," July 15, 1969, pp. 12-14.)

HARTMAN RECTOR, JR.

"Close Enough to the Angels"

President Dyer came across the hall and said, "President McKay would like to see you two brethren right away." And so we went across to the Hotel Utah and up to President McKay's suite and into a little waiting room and met Sister Middlemiss.

She said, "You're Brother Rector, and you're Brother Dunn [Loren C. Dunn]."

"Yes."

"President McKay would like to see you first, Brother Rector."

And so I went with President Dyer into the Prophet's office, and there I saw the Prophet, with that wonderful President McKay smile, the white hair, those penetrating blue eyes. I knew that I was standing in the presence of a prophet of God—there was no doubt in my mind. And there wouldn't have been any doubt in anyone's mind, whether they were a member of the Church or not. He is the prophet on earth today.

He said, "Brother Rector?" I took his hand, and I told him how much it meant to me, a newcomer into the kingdom, to shake hands with the prophet. He smiled and said, "Brother Rector, will you accept a call to the First Council of the Seventy?"

Now if I had been expecting that, I guess I could have understood it. But as it was I said, "What?"

He said, "I want you to serve as one of the General Authorities of the Church."

I said, "President McKay, do you mean am I worthy to serve as one of the General Authorities?

He said, "No, no, no." I guess he decided to see if he

186

could get through to me some other way. He said, "Do you know who died recently of the General Authorities?"

I said, "Yes, President Antoine R. Ivins."

He said, "Yes, I want *you* to take *his place.*"

Then I understood what the Prophet had asked me. I probably said something very trite, for I said "President McKay, I could never take his place, but I might fill the vacancy. And if you and the Lord want me to fill this position, yes, yes, I will accept it,"—not knowing fully what I was saying, I'm sure.

He smiled and settled back in his chair. President Dyer came in and said, "President McKay, this man has a wonderful aunt (that was his recommendation for me), and he converted her, too." Well I *do* have a wonderful aunt. I said, "President, I did baptize her, but I didn't convert her; she has always been converted, I'm sure."

President McKay, with a twinkle in his eye, said, "Well, President Dyer, he's a good man too!" And then he took my hand again and said, "Brother Rector, I want you to know that the Lord loves you, and that we love you too. And we are delighted that you are going to be serving with us."

I thanked him and told him how much he has meant to us (particularly the brethren in the Church). Among other things, he has taught us how to love our wives. President McKay is the greatest example of gallant manhood that I know anything about. If you want to know how to treat your wife, or mother, or your fiance, you must treat them like the Prophet treats Sister Emma Riggs McKay. And that will be close enough to the angels.

(*Speeches of the Year*, "Get Yourself In Condition to Serve," Oct. 1, 1968, pp. 13-14.)

HARTMAN RECTOR, JR.

"My Spirit Is Nine Feet Tall"

Now the thing that normally stands before and between us and our accomplishments in this life is our weaknesses. If I asked you where you got your weaknesses, how would you answer that question? Some will say that they are responsible for their own weaknesses, that we make a lot of mistakes—we keep adding to the list of weaknesses. But that answer would not be strictly correct.

Others would answer, "Well, from Mom and Dad—you know, heredity." Their weaknesses come from their parents. We hear a lot about heredity. It is very convenient—We can always blame things on mom and dad. And yet that answer would not be strictly true either.

Well then, how about environment? There is a lot of information available to show that environment pretty much determines what we are going to be. And there are a lot of people who obviously believe this and use it as an excuse for their weaknesses. But when you come right down to it, where *do* you get your weaknessess? You will find the answer on page 502 in the Book of Mormon.

All the answers are in this book. I have never found a question whose answer could not be found in here. They are all in here [the Book of Mormon].

I started to read the Book of Mormon shortly before I met the missionaries in my home. Then I went into a Sunday School investigator's class in San Diego. The teacher of that class was a little man five feet, two inches tall, by the name of Joseph Smith Wilson. Joseph Smith Wilson had been dedicated to preach the gospel by his mother before he was born. She lived over in Scotland—married to a nonmember, a drunkard, who beat her and beat the children. She made a covenant with the Lord that if he would give her a son she would dedicate him to preaching the gospel and send him to Zion. Her husband ridiculed her and laughed at her—said that she couldn't have a son; but she did. You see, the Lord recognized that covenant with that good sister. She had a son, and she named him Joseph Smith Wilson. And when he was nineteen years old she kissed him goodbye for the last time, put him on a ship, sent him to Salt Lake City, and never saw him again in her life. She literally gave her son to preach the gospel of Jesus Christ.

Well he was true to that charge. I believe he is one of the greatest living authorities on the Book of Mormon. As I attended his class I had lots of questions that I was going to ask. I had been looking for the answers all my life and hadn't been too successful in finding them. So I would ask him my questions. He would say, "Brother Rector, that is on page 127," and he would turn to page 127 and read me the answer. I would say, "That's interesting, now what about this?" He would say, "That's on page 232," and he would turn to page 232 and read me the answer.

Tremendous individual, this. As I said, he is five feet two. He used to say, "My body is very small (he kept his Scottish accent, he liked it) but my spirit is nine feet tall." And it is!

(*Speeches of the Year,* Get Yourself in Condition to Serve," Oct. 1, 1968, pp. 4-5.)

HARTMAN RECTOR, JR.

"It Is What's Inside That Really Counts"

I am sure as I look into your faces here—and this is an awesome sight for me, looking into the faces of all you tremendous, young Latter-day Saints and other friends—I approach you with fear and trembling, to say the least. But you are the best looking group in the world—I know that. Not so much because of the way you wear your hair or the clothes you wear or the way you dress, but it is what is inside that really counts. There is a cigarette ad or slogan like that, isn't there? "It's what's inside that counts." Well it *is* what's inside that really counts.

My grandmother was worried about my religious training at an early age, as most grandmothers are. So she took it upon herself to read me the Bible every time I went to visit her. As she read, she always added her own interpretations. She said, "Pretty is as pretty does. Beauty is only skin deep (she firmly believed that); it is what's inside that really makes you beautiful." The comic Andy Griffith has added, "but ugliness goes clean through to the bone."

It is what's inside that determines the way you are going to look. Abe Lincoln knew this. One time when a vacancy existed in his cabinet, he was encouraged to appoint a certain man to fill that vacancy by one of his other cabinet members. Abe demurred, he wasted time, he procrastinated; he did everything but appoint the man. And finally Stanton became outdone with him and said, "Mr. President, are you going to appoint this man or aren't you?" And Abe said, "No, I'm not going to appoint him." Stanton said, "Why not? He is a good man, isn't he?" Abe said, "I don't like his face." (Imagine Abe Lincoln not liking someone's face! Ever have a look at Abe's face? Abe was homely as all get-out, but he was beautiful because of what was inside of him.) And Stanton said, "You don't like his face! What kind of a reason is that for not appointing a man?" Abe said something I think pretty well depicted his attitude. He said, "Any man who is forty years old is responsible for what his face looks like." And that is true. By that age our countenances disclose the kind of person we *really* are *inside*. It is what's inside that really counts.

(Speeches of the Year, "Get Yourself in Condition to Serve," Oct. 1, 1968, pp. 2-3.)

HARTMAN RECTOR, JR.

"He Really Passed the Test"

I had a friend, one time, who went to take a test in school, a test for which he had not studied. Of course he had prayed pretty hard about it. He had asked the Lord to help him remember something he had not bothered to learn. There are some things the Lord cannot do. Other things he can, but he will not. And praying will not work in these cases. I know; I have tried it. But as this friend went in to take this test, he found he was sitting right next to the smartest girl in the class. He said, "Well, this must be the answer to my prayer. Here she is. The Lord provided her, right here." But he was a returned missionary. He had been preaching honesty for two years. It is very difficult to go against that which you have been preaching and for which you have had a witness of the Spirit. While he was arguing with himself about what he was going to do on this test, he flunked the test. But as a matter of fact he really passed.

You see, he had passed the Lord's test, and that is the test that we have to pass here upon this earth. Tests are all around us. Fifty years from the day that he took the test he would not remember what his grade was, and it really would not make any difference so long as it was honest. But if he cheated on the test, he would remember that, for it makes an indelible imprint on the spirit. It also makes it easier the next time we are faced with a temptation where our honesty is in question to go down that "broad road." Lucifer would not dare tempt you with a sin as grievous as robbing a bank with your first experience with dishonesty. That would turn you off. You would not dare do that. So he will start with something small, something little, something that seems insignificant. If you flunk that one, he will see to it that you get a larger one and than a larger one, until it reaches the point where some people can sit down and methodically work out a plan to rob a bank. Oh, they will rationalize some justification for it, such as, "It is insured by the government so nobody is losing anything." Or, "Well, I really have it coming to me; I have not had the breaks that other people have." This called rationalization, which is a form of lying to yourself. But it is lying, nevertheless. As Nephi said: ". . . And thus the devil cheateth their souls, and leadeth them away carefully down to hell." (2 Nephi 28:21.)

(Speeches of the Year, "Get Up and Glow," January 5, 1971, p. 7.)

HARTMAN RECTOR, JR.

"You Do It If You Are Going to Be Honest"

Brother Sterling W. Sill tells an interesting story about buying a bottle of pop. He was driving down the road and got thirsty, so he stopped to buy some pop. He put a dime in the pop machine at the filling station and got a bottle of pop, but his dime was returned. He took the dime out, looked at it, put it in his pocket, started back to the car, and said, "They charge too much for this stuff anyway." But he did not quite get back to the car, because there was a still, small voice that shouted in his ear and asked him a very interesting question. The question was "Sill, are you really going to be a thief for ten cents?" Well, no, of course he was not going to be a thief for ten cents. Who would? The price is not nearly high enough. So, he went back to the pop machine and started to put the dime back in. But now he had a problem. If he put the dime in the pop machine, what would happen? He would get another bottle of pop. Right? He might even get his dime back. This would sort of "compound the fracture." What would you do in a situation like that? You might figure that this just too big a problem for me to solve. The Lord would not expect me to solve this problem. You can get a clue as to what you should do by considering what you would do if you had put a dime in the pop machine and you did not get a bottle of pop. After you got through kicking and shaking and beating on the machine, you would probably go to the filling station attendant and say, "Look, that machine is a thief; it robbed me. I want my money back."

This is what Brother Sill did: he gave his dime to the filling station attendant who, of course, thought he was crazy, because you just do not do things like that. But you do if you are going to be honest. Did you ever stop as you were walking past a telephone booth and pull down the little coin box and look in? Did you ever do that? What were you looking for? And if you found a whole box full of money there, what would you say about that? Would you think, "Oh, the Lord provided for me." You see, if you are not careful, you will try to give the Lord credit for things that he does not want to take credit for. And that you have to watch always.

(*Speeches of the Year*, "Get Up and Glow," January 5, 1971, pp. 6-7.)

HARTMAN RECTOR, JR.

"A Tower of Strength"

I have witnessed this . . . truth in force today. While I was serving as a stake mission president at one time, the missionaries were meeting with a very good man who was not a member of the Church, but who was married to a fine Latter-day Saint sister. This good brother wanted to join the Church, but he was addicted to tobacco. He had tried to quit many times, but he said he couldn't; he was just too weak.

There were six stake missionaries who had met with him over a considerable period of time but who were unable to help him develop the strength to quit smoking. Finally, under the influence of the Spirit, we asked him if we could fast with him that he might overcome this weakness. He considered the offer and agreed to our proposal. We asked him then if he would carry out the fast for *two days.* He agreed, so the fast went forth. Six stake missionaries, the smoking brother, and his wife fasted.

At the completion of the fast, we all met in his home and knelt with him in his living room, each praying in turn. The prayers were essentially the same; they were, that the Lord would take from this brother his desire to smoke. He was the last to pray and then he arose and announced, "I have no desire to smoke." He hasn't smoked unto this day. Since that time he has served in the bishopric of his ward and even now is serving in a stake MIA superintendency. He is today a stalwart in the faith, a real servant of the Lord. The Lord literally took from him his weakness and made him a tower of strength instead. This he will always do when we come unto him and have faith in him. He will turn our weaknesses into strengths.

(*Conference Report,* April 1970, pp. 140-41.)

HARTMAN RECTOR, JR.

"He Reached for the Cigarette"

Our Heavenly Father wants us to be free; he doesn't want us to be in bondage to our appetites and passions. Therefore, he has given us commandments that are only calculated to make us free. And he tells us that all of his commandments are spiritual. [See D&C 29:34.] Never at any time has he given a commandment that is not spiritual. Even the Word of Wisdom is a spiritual commandment in that it primarily effects our spirits, and certainly it does.

To illustrate, I knew a man who was a member of the Church but had returned to his habit of smoking cigarettes. He said he didn't want to smoke but just couldn't help it. Of course, he could have overcome the habit if he had really wanted to while he had his body to help him. If the spirit tells the body not to pick up the cigarette, the body won't pick it up, and abstinence over time allows the spirit to overcome the desire.

This man finally suffered a stroke. His body was paralyzed with the exception of his right arm and his eyes. As his son-in-law picked him up from the porch of his house, where he'd fallen, with the only arm this man could move, he reached for the cigarette in his son-in-law's mouth. But he could not hold onto it. His son-in-law held the lighted cigarette to the stricken man's lips, but in his condition he could not hold it in his mouth.

For nine months this man lay on his bed. He actually wore out the pocket of his pajamas reaching into it for a cigarette that was not there. Then he died and went into the spirit world. Do you suppose he still wants a cigarette? On the basis of Amulek's statement, he does. But there is just one catch—there are no cigarettes in the spirit world. Would you suppose he is in paradise or in spirit prison? The answer seems only too obvious.

(Conference Report, October 1970, p. 74.)

Biographical Sketch

BISHOP ROBERT L. SIMPSON

Robert L. Simpson, first counselor in the Presiding Bishopric of The Church of Jesus Christ of Latter-day Saints, has had wide experience in business and in Church administration. He is married to the former Jelaire Chandler of Los Angeles, and they have three children—two boys and a girl.

A native of Salt Lake City, he spent much of his life in Southern California where he made his home until called to the Presiding Bishopric in October of 1961.

Bishop Simpson was president of the New Zealand Mission (1958-1961) where he had served previously as a missionary before World War II. He also has served in a ward bishopric, on a stake high council, as a stake mission president, as a stake YMMIA superintendent, and as a seminary instructor; and he was the servicemen's coordinator for the Church in North Africa and the Middle East while serving as a captain in the Air Force, 1943-1945.

In business, Bishop Simpson was with the Pacific Telephone Company for twenty years, being successively a plant engineer, public relations supervisor, and supervisor of an accounting office when named to the Presiding Bishopric.

Bishop Simpson received his formal schooling in Southern California, graduating from the Santa Monica City College.

His special interests include studies of the Maori culture and sports. Currently he serves as first vice-chairman of the board of trustees of the Health Services Corporation of The Church of Jesus Christ of Latter-day Saints; member of the National Cubbing Committee, Boy Scouts of America; member of the executive board for Region 12 and member of the executive board of the Great Salt Lake Council of Boy Scouts of America.

ROBERT L. SIMPSON

"Just a Few Pennies a Day"

I would like to tell you also of an experience I had down in New Zealand, going into a humble Maori home. Here we had a situation where a mother and father and twelve children were living the gospel as well as anyone I have ever seen in all my life. As they would gather around each evening to have their family devotional scripture readings and have the children participate, there was a time in the evening when the father would put a few pennies in a glass jar sitting upon the mantle. The house was lighted with candles and kerosene lamps. In this humble home this little jar was always there—just a few pennies each day. This was their family temple fund. (Imagine a family of fourteen trying to save a few pennies a day, knowing that they would have to travel thousands of miles, at least to Hawaii, in order to get to the House of the Lord to do what they wanted to do.) Then they would kneel down in prayer, and from the smallest child they would take their turns and ask Heavenly Father that they might enjoy the rich blessing of having their family sealed together in order that they might have the fulness of the gospel come into their home.

I used to sit there and literally break up inside wondering how these wonderful people would ever realize this blessing. A few pennies a day—they just could not possibly get a family of fourteen to the temple on a few pennies a day, and I did not know how they could ever do it. But they prayed in great faith, and they prayed with devotion, and they meant what they said.

If someone had told me at that time that within my lifetime there would be a temple built within sixty miles of this very home, I would have said, "I don't believe it," because I did not have the same faith these people had. I am not sure that they visualized the building of a temple in New Zealand either, but they knew that their family was going to get together and be sealed and receive the rich blessings of the gospel. I want to tell you that the Lord is mindful of these people. He was mindful of their plea, and he poured his blessings out upon this family—and this family was multiplied by many hundreds throughout the length and breadth of New Zealand. It is a wonderful thing to contemplate the great blessings of the Lord to these Polynesian people as he listens to their prayers of faith.

(*Speeches of the Year,* "The Lord Is Mindful of His Own," April 4 1962, pp. 8-9.)

ROBERT L. SIMPSON

"*Charting a Course*"

Victor Hugo once commented, and I quote: "When the disposal of time is surrendered to the chance of incidents—chaos will reign." And, young people, truer words were never spoken.

Let me tell you about a missionary who felt the need for charting a course. He wanted to put a little guarantee in his charted course, so this is what he did. He wrote down for himself his major objectives for the next five years. He called it his "five-year plan." On this five-year plan, I remember, he had such entries as an honorable release from his mission (which was then just starting). He had as an objective graduating with a particular grade-point average (which was quite high, I might add). Within that five-year period he hoped to be married in the House of the Lord (and he had a pretty good idea who it was going to be). I also remember he had a notation about continuing worthily in the Church while he was achieving all of these things—worthy with regard to tithing, the Word of Wisdom, attendance at sacrament meetings, being available to his bishop, being a home teacher or whatever else might need to be done which would be compatible with his busy schedule, and doing all those things that a good Latter-day Saint should do.

Now comes the important part. Having prepared this list, he made about five or six copies, with plenty of room at the bottom for additional signatures. Then he had witnesses to these objectives that he had set; he had his parents, his mission president and wife (we were greatly honored to do this), his bishop back home, and his athletic coach (whom he respected very highly), all signed as witnesses to these commitments that he had made for himself. He was the kind of boy that would not want to disappoint those whom he loved. He would want to do these things so he would not have to say to all of us, "I failed."

I can tell you now that this young man has accomplished his goals. He is ready now to take his place in the world. He feels prepared to meet whatever comes next, and, most important of all, he has already prepared a brand-new set of goals that is going to carry him for the next five years, during the struggling days of beginning his business. And I would like to state right here that I know he will make it because he has established sound goals and has the self-discipline to pursue them effectively.

(*Speeches of the Year*, "Organizing for Eternity," April 20, 1965, p. 4.)

ROBERT L. SIMPSON

"This Young Lady Was Loyal"

Now if I may be personal for a minute or two, may I tell you that one of the greatest blessings of my life has been an eternal companionship with my sweetheart. When I was just about your age, we were having an M Men and Gleaner conference in Southern California. I had been the first speaker, representing the young men, and while I was speaking some dignitary came and occupied my seat on the stand. Upon concluding my talk, I sat on the front row in the congregation, and then they introduced the Gleaner representative. As she talked I became very, very interested in what she was saying. I can't tell you a word she said, but I know *how* she said it, and I know the *spirit* that was there. And I decided right then and there, "This is a young lady that I would like to get to know better."

Well, we had some dates. And you know, on that first date, I didn't even have enough money to take her to a show, and shows only cost thirty-five cents in those days. We walked up and down Hollywood Boulevard (of all places) and we looked in the windows and we chatted. We communicated, and I found out some of the things that she liked and believed in and she found out about some of the things I liked and believed in, and they were amazingly similar. Then we dated some more, and finally it was time to become engaged.

During these months of dating, it was a rich experience. It was during these dating opportunities that I observed one or two very important things. It might even sound silly, but I would take her to a show—when I finally got thirty-five cents I would take her to a show and she always cried in the right places. Now doesn't that sound foolish? But this impressed me; she always cried in the right places, just to the right degree. And when it was humorous she laughed in the right places, but she did it in a controlled way, and this pleased me and impressed me.

Then I noticed that this young lady was loyal. She was loyal to her family, she was loyal to the old high school she used to go to (and they were our arch rivals and I didn't see how anyone could be loyal to that school, but she was). She was even loyal to UCLA—she was a student at UCLA. And she was loyal to the Church. I thought to myself, "She has a built-in capacity for loyalty." And I said, "If she is loyal to all these things, if she accepts me to be her companion, she will be loyal to me. No question about it." And that is exactly the way it has been.

Young people, what a great blessing when we take time to do it in the Lord's appointed way; when we don't rush these things; when we look earnestly, prayerfully; when we communicate and find out what is way down deep inside. This is what we must do, because choosing an eternal companion wisely will be just as important as was the acquisition of a mortal body or going into the waters of baptism, for without that eternal companion there will be no exaltation. The celestial kingdom? Could be. But exaltation? Only with that eternal companion who believes as you believe, who feels as you feel, who shares with you an abiding faith and testimony in God, His Son, and the power of the priesthood.

(*Speeches of the Year* "Eternity Is Serious Business," September 30, 1969, pp. 7-8.)

ROBERT L. SIMPSON

"Right into My Hands"

May I tell you that I have had a glorious summer. May I tell you that during this summer I had thrilling experiences as I contacted people all over these United States who were excited about what the Church is doing. One man in particular just unwittingly fell right into my hands. We were seated in an aircraft going from Chicago down to Miami and he started talking about politics.

He said, "You know, I think President Nixon is doing a tremendous job." And he said, "The thing that thrills me most is the fact that he has surrounded himself with really religious competent men. You take this man Romney, for example. Why he has just been chosen the Churchman of the Year in America. Now," he said, "that is the kind of men we need running this country."

And I said, "Well, did you happen to know that he was a Mormon?"

"Yes, I knew that."

And I said, "Well, I happen to be a Mormon too."

And he said, "Well, that's interesting."

I went on to tell him about Ezra Taft Benson and other great men in Washington who had filled similar roles, and he said, "Well, they're not all Mormons." He said, "There is another great churchman on President Nixon's cabinet, but he must be a Catholic because his name is Kennedy."

And I said, "Well, you're probably talking about the Secretary of the Treasury. He happens to have been our stake president in Chicago before he had this role."

He just couldn't believe that until I finally convinced him. Then they served lunch on the airplane, and as they put the meal before us and while we were enjoying it, he said, "You know, the man that prepares all these meals for the airlines also took charge of President Nixon's inauguration, and he is a great spiritual man."

I said, "You must be talking about Willard Marriott."

He said, "Yes, how did you know the name?"

I said, "Well, he happens to have been our stake president in Washington, D.C."

Everyone he mentioned just happened to be a tremendous member of the Church, and we had a great conversation all the way down to Miami.

(*Speeches of the Year,* "Eternity Is Serious Business," September 30, 1969, pp. 1-2.)

ROBERT L. SIMPSON

"You Are Going to Jump Up and Down"

Let me attempt to create a picture in your mind's eye.

Suppose you were standing on a beautiful green hill. Can you see the picture now? It is springtime. The grass is green; the trees are beautiful. The day is perfect. The temperature is just right. There is a gentle breeze blowing. You feel like the world is at your command. You are all alone on this hill. You see this beautiful, peaceful river as it winds around the hill. My, what a beautiful sight it is!

But as you turn around and look on the back side of the hill, you notice this beautiful, peaceful river drops over an abrupt waterfall and crashes onto some rocks at the bottom. Then all of a sudden you hear music. You hear voices. It sounds familiar. You look back, and right down there on that same river is a boat with about eight or ten of your friends. One is playing a guitar; all are singing together. They are truly enjoying life as they allow the current to take them downstream. You say, "My, isn't that delightful! How I would like to be with them!" There they are, just drifting, not knowing where the river is going to take them.

Then all of a sudden it dawns on you—the waterfall! The jagged rocks at the bottom! What are you going to do, young people? Will you just fold your arms and say, "Now, this should be interesting. Let's see what happens here." You are not going to do that, are you? You are going to jump up and down; you are going to shout; you are going to get excited about it.

That is exactly what we do. We do a little jumping up and down, and we get excited, because, young people, we know where the jagged rocks and pitfalls are. Our prophets have told and continue to tell us the things that we should do as well as the areas to avoid in order that we might get back into the presence of our Heavenly Father.

So as we who love you get excited, as we raise our voices, as we wave our arms, would you forgive us, please; and would you just know it is because we love you so much. We don't want you to get into any situation that would not be a blessing to you. We want to be with you when the greatest day of your life or our lives comes—when we feel that friendly arm on our shoulders and the kindly voice of someone who is over all, as He says, "Well done, thou good and faithful servant. . . . enter thou into the joy of thy lord." (Matthew 25:21.)

I bear you my testimony that this gospel is true. God lives, and Jesus is the Christ. We have guideposts to follow, and only by following these things that have been set down can we hope to gain the rewards that are there for us.

(*Speeches of the Year*, "Do Your Standards Show?," October 19, 1965, pp. 10-11.)

ROBERT L. SIMPSON

"It Sounded True, It Sounded Real"

Let me tell you about a good man in California a few years ago. He would stand on fast and testimony Sunday and bear a fine testimony. He would tell us how he would willingly give his life for the Church when the persecutions come upon us again—*someday*. It sounded true, it sounded real. Then we would meet this good brother out in the foyer afterward and shake his hand and thank him for sharing his testimony with us. We would say something like, "Now, Brother So-and-so, how about home teaching next Tuesday night?" "Well," he would reply, "I am sorry, but I have been watching 'Gunsmoke' on Tuesday nights, and I will not be able to make it. But some day I am going to give my life for this great Church, some day I am going to make the great sacrifice, but I cannot be available next Tuesday night. I have some personal interests to take care of!"

My dear young friends, you know as well as I that when that someday might come, this good man will not be available to his Heavenly Father. He will not be standing in defense of what he believes, because he will perhaps have a personal interest that will take priority.

(*Speeches of the Year*, "Gifts of the Spirit," October 18, 1966, p. 8.)

R O B E R T   L .   S I M P S O N

"The Game of Life"

Speaking of television, last Monday night my high-school-age son persuaded me to sit down and watch the second half of a football game. I have always made it a policy that no sacrifice is too great for my boy. So we sat down and watched football. While watching this game, some facts became very apparent. In fact, it had gospel application and priesthood application.

I noticed, for example, that there were no shortcuts to the goal line. It was a hundred yards in both directions. I also noticed that the team that seemed to have had the most practice, that did the best planning, that executed their plays the best, and that had the best team attitude, was the team that made the most points.

I also noticed that when team members cooperated and helped one another, the team made the most yardage.

It was also obvious that when someone broke the rules, there was always a penalty imposed. It sounds a lot like life, doesn't it? In talking about this to my boy, he said, "Fifteen yards is nothing; but, Dad, when you ground me for three days, that is too much."

We also noticed that no one was allowed to make up his own rules as the game progressed. They all lost their free agency to do that when they agreed to join the team and play according to the established rules.

And last but not least, I noticed when it was all over, the winning team was a lot happier than the team that lost.

Now brethren, we believe that "men are, that they might have joy"; and joy can best come as we obtain victory in the game of life, played according to the only acceptable rules—those set down by our Heavenly Father.

(*Conference Report*, October 1970, pp. 98-99.)

Robert L. Simpson

ROBERT L. SIMPSON

"Were You On Noah's Ark?"

I guess the only disconcerting thing about coming down here is to be with all of the youth and feel that each year I am a year older than I was last time. I think President Hugh B. Brown said it best of all when he told us a little story a few weeks ago; maybe you heard it. He told of having his little grandson on his knee. The boy looked up at President Brown with the admiration of a great grandson. Finally, he put his hand up and felt some of the wrinkles in President Brown's face. Then he reached up and stroked President Brown's beautiful white hair. Then the little grandson said, "Grandpa Brown, were you on Noah's ark?" And President Brown replied, "No, son, Grandaddy Brown wasn't on Noah's ark." And the little boy looked up and said, "Well, how come you weren't drowned?"

(*Speeches of the Year*, "The Church Is Alive," November 3, 1970, p. 2.)

ROBERT L. SIMPSON

"Be a Good Receiver"

To accomplish today's purpose, you and I must feel something. There needs to be an interaction

211

between us. That interaction can best come about as we communicate effectively. For the next few minutes I would like to play the role of a transmitter in our two-way communication system. You will be the receiver. Like any transmitter, my power supply must be adequate and properly regulated. My vacuum tubes and intricate connections should all be in order; and provided that my antenna is capable of a good clear signal, there is an excellent chance of a satisfactory transmission going out.

Now my transmission is useless unless there are receivers that are plugged in, on frequency, and anxiously tuned in with listening ears and hearts, all ready to evaluate, analyze, and most important of all, to react to what is said. Only then can our time be best spent.

The world seems forever plagued with a lack of understanding between nations. Traditionally we humans have been without the ability to communicate well across international borders. Our very own nation within the past couple of years has been torn by vicious riots, partly because large and important factions of our citizenry are failing in their ability to communicate with one another. Oh, true enough, the transmissions have been loud and clear—but sometimes I wonder what has happened to the receivers. We only seem to listen to and hear that which we want to.

Perhaps saddest of all is the fact that family units, the basic and most important of all units in our social order, seem to be breaking up by the thousands each week—all because husbands and wives, parents and children, or next-door neighbors, find it difficult to establish a simple and clear line of communication between them.

The greatest need in the world today is for the gospel of Jesus Christ. The greatest challenge you and I have as the custodians of this truth is the ability to communicate better with a world that needs what we have.

Now for the sake of interest and to start some thought processes in motion, come with me for a minute as we roll back the calendar about a hundred years. By contrast, we can best contemplate the miracle of communication in our time.

Robert L. Simpson

Too often we take for granted the convenience and ease of today's methods of communication. From these very hills that surround this Utah Valley in which we meet this morning, Indian smoke signals could be seen less than a hundred years ago as messages were sent across the miles to signal the success or failure of a hunting party or perhaps the approach of a covered wagon train. Yes, after thousands of years there had been few advances in the field of communication. Jungle drums, tom toms, smoke signals, and—oh yes—we mustn't forget the revolutionary new Pony Express of that day. But all this seemed to be about the best the mind of man was capable of after all that time.

An interesting sidelight of United States history suggests the ingenuity and the inventive genius of 1825 as the top brains of that day were employed to devise a sure and quick way of notifying the population of New York City about the departure of the first barge from Albany as it headed down the newly completed Erie Canal. The canal was a historic feat. It provided a new avenue of commerce and trade from the Great Lakes to New York City. All the citizenry of New York, some 430 miles downstream, were eager to start a giant celebration as the new waterway was officially declared in operation with the departure of this first barge.

Now this urgent need for a better way of communicating was solved as follows: 43 cannons from the War of 1812 were stationed ten miles apart along the length of the Erie Canal. As the barge entered the canal, cannon number one fired; nearly a minute later, the attendant of cannon number two heard the sound, and he lit the fuse and cannon number two was fired; and so the sound was relayed until all 43 cannons had been fired in rotation. At last the people in New York heard the report of the last cannon, and at that instant the celebration was underway. Total elapsed time for the message—approximately one hour. It had to go 430 miles.

You see, sound travels slowly—only about 740 miles per hour. As a matter of fact, if we had a hollow tube telephone system in this country, with some means of propagating our voices through the tube instead of allowing our voice patterns to ride piggy back on electromagnetic waves, our California students here at the "Y" when calling home would shout "Hello" into the mouthpiece, and that hello would take about one hour to travel to the coast. Then mom or dad would shout back "Hello," and that's right, two hours have gone by and all you have said is "Hello." The only thing worse than the service would be the bill, especially if it were going to be at today's rates.

Let me give you one more interesting contrast in comparing the speed of sound with electromagnetic waves. The next time you watch a World Series baseball game on TV and see the batter hit a long fly ball to center field, just remember that the sound of the bat hitting the ball hops into a microphone not far from home plate and then speeds on electromagnetic waves directly into your living room. That speed is 186,000 miles per second—about $7\frac{1}{2}$ times around this earth in one short second. The center fielder in the ball park has had to wait for those lumbering slow sound waves to reach him some 300 feet away; and although he will probably catch the ball, TV viewers in California, perhaps 3,000 miles away, heard the crack of the bat before he did. All of this is made possible through the miracle of our modern-day electrical communication.

Well now, young people, we are living in a great day; and we read and hear about coaxial cables; we hear about microwave radio relay systems; we hear about earth-orbiting satellites, moon robots talking back to earth, and even "hot lines" between heads of nations, providing us with an absolute miracle of communication from a pure technological and mechanical standpoint. But as a world filled with more than three billion people, we are failing miserably in our ability to really get the message through. I think we can conlude that the source of our failure is human. It stems from the uncompromising, the selfish—yes, even at times the deceitful heart and mind of man. No one, in my opinion, can be a good transmitter unless he has *first learned to be a good receiver.*

One of the great communication problems of our day is the communication of empty words—just *words,* no real message, no stimulus for thought. As children of our Heavenly Father, he would have us *say* something as we give utterance, and that is what we would like to talk about here today.

Any person who reads and understands the scriptures is better prepared to speak with wisdom. How glorious that we have a divine, uncontaminated source of light and knowledge.

(*Speeches of the Year*, "If You Would Communicate Well," October 13, 1964, pp. 2-4.)

ROBERT L. SIMPSON

"Welfare Work in Action"

Let me tell you about a wonderful bishop up in Logan who caught the vision of the bishop's youth council committee, who communicated with his young people. His young people were tired of going and hoeing weeds at the welfare farm. They wanted to have a more realistic welfare experience. They wanted to do something that was meaningful in their lives. And so he said, "All right, you tell me what you would like to do." These young people put their heads together, and they said, "Bishop, you give us a list of all the shut-ins in our ward. You give us a list of all the people who are alone and cannot get out to sacrament meeting. We are going to spend our Friday nights for the next few months going into these homes. We are going to prepare their dinner for them. We are going to put on a little program after dinner. We would like to have a testimony meeting with them, and then the priests would like to administer the sacrament."

Here we have these young people up in Logan who are willing to go out and bless the shut-ins of their community. You talk about welfare work in action. This was their idea. This is what they wanted to do. This is how they wanted to interpret the teachings of the Savior in their lives.

(*Speeches of the Year*, "The Church Is Alive," November 3, 1970, p. 6.)

ROBERT L. SIMPSON

"Good Samaritan"

We had another group of young people who got all of the people of the ward to come out on a Saturday morning. The youth lined themselves up in front of the recreation hall. They had the big ones at one end, the medium size, then the shorter ones. Then they said, "Now brothers and sisters, you all have something that needs to be done, and we are just the people who can do it for you. The big ones are two dollars an hour, the medium size are a dollar-and-a-half, and the shorter ones are a dollar an hour." They had a slave market, and they went out as slaves for the people. They could have them for two hours or ten hours, and they did their work. They came back with four or five hundred dollars. It was a tremendous thing to see all of these young people involved in doing something for someone else. It was a tremendous thing!

What was at the root of it all? A prophet of God and vision and revelation and inspiration of our day. All of these things are happening all over the Church.

Let me tell you just one more thing before I close about this project called "Good Samaritan." Reverend Givens came to a banquet as we culminated "Project Good Samaritan." We were going to announce how much money had been raised. He had his leaders from California there. One leader from California was just amazed; and as he looked down on President Smith and President Lee and the rest of us assembled there, including many stake presidents and their wives, he said, "Why this is one of the most glorious things I have ever seen. We are united; we are together. You have done something for us and we needed it; we are so grateful to you." He said, "Now one thing I want to plea for here tonight. Let's not let the outside world come in now and put us at one another's throats. We have accomplished something here that is tremendous. And we can see one another as true brothers and sisters under our Heavenly Father. Let's not let the outside world come now and put us at one another's throats."

You know, they had a choir singing that night from this black congregation. They sang two songs. The words in the first song went like this: "Please don't move that mountain, but give me strength to climb it."

If the minority groups in the world need to learn one thing, it is the message of this song: "Please don't move that mountain, but give me strength to climb it."

That is exactly what we were trying to do for these people on that occasion. Then the other song they sang went like this: "Something in the way He moves lets me know He's my friend."

I think they were trying to tell us something and I hope that they will always consider us as their friends.

A little by-product of this "Project Good Samaritan": about two weeks later, Reverend Givens invited me to come over to their area church conference. They were having a regional conference of this three-million-member church, about the same size as ours. But these few hundred assembled were from this particular area. They had a special guest at that conference, the head of all their women's auxiliaries, the counterpart to Sister Belle Spafford of our Church, president of the Relief

Society. As I talked to them, I concluded with this thought, "I want to tell you one more thing. If you really want to be blessed and you really want to be happy, why don't you designate one night a week, and circle your calendar, and have all your family together on that night without fail. You might want to read a few scriptures, and maybe your children can respond on some of the things they have been taught at school. Then you can conduct some of your family business. Afterwards you may want to have some refreshments and play a few games together and just have a good family circle. Then you can have your family prayer together before the hour is over. You might want to call it something like the 'Family Home Evening.'" As I finished, this woman stood up and said, "Reverend Givens, I've got one more thing to say." She came over to the microphone and said, "Brothers and Sisters, I have been taught all my life never to be a copycat; but I want to tell you, from this night on, I'm going to be a copycat. Because everyone in this church is going to hear about the 'Family Home Evening.'"

When people hear the truth, and when they hear something that has come from Heavenly Father through his prophets, they recognize it as truth. They seem to know that it is something that is eternal, that it will bring blessings to their lives. Oh, what a wonderful thing it is to see the Church recognized by other good people.

(*Speeches of the Year*, "The Church Is Alive," November 3, 1970, pp. 7-8.)

ROBERT L. SIMPSON

"But Daddy, I Wasn't Talking to You"

As a child of God kneels to pray, that individual must believe implicitly that his prayer is being heard by him to whom the prayer is addressed. The thought that our Heavenly Father is too busy to, that our message is being recorded by celestial computers for possible future consideration, is unthinkable and inconsistent with all we have been taught by his holy prophets.

It was thrilling to listen to a father relate this story about his three-year-old youngster recently, as they knelt by the crib in the usual manner for the little fellow to say his simple bedtime prayer. Eyes closed, heads bowed, seconds passed, and there were no words spoken by the child. Just about the time Dad was going to open his eyes to check the lengthy delay, little Tommy was on his feet and climbing into bed. "How about your prayers?" asked Dad.

"I said my prayers," came the reply.

"But son, Daddy didn't hear you."

Then followed the child's classic statement: "But Daddy, I wasn't talking to you."

Even three-year-olds have personal, private matters to discuss with Heavenly Father from time to time.

(*Conference Report*, April 1970, p. 89.)

Biographical Sketch

PATRIARCH ELDRED G. SMITH

Elder Eldred G. Smith is the seventh Patriarch to The Church of Jesus Christ of Latter-day Saints and is the great-great-great-grandson of Joseph Smith Sr., first Patriarch to the Church and father of Joseph Smith Jr., prophet-founder of the Church.

Elder Smith was born January 9, 1907, in Lehi, Utah, son of Hyrum G. and Martha Gee Smith. When his father became presiding Patriarch to the Church (this is the only office in the Church that follows the patriarchal line from father to son), the family moved to Salt Lake City, where young Eldred was educated in the public schools, the old Latter-day Saints High School, and the University of Utah.

His first call to Church service was as a missionary to the Swiss-German Mission, 1926-1929. Later Church positions included a stake mission in Liberty Stake, 1929-1932, and a term as member of the stake board of the Mutual Improvement Association in the Ensign Stake for a year and a half from November 1936. From that position he was chosen to serve as second counselor in the bishopric of the 20th Ward, May 25, 1938. On March 10, 1940 the stake was divided, and Elder

Smith was named a member of the high council, serving until February 16, 1941, when he was sustained bishop of the newly created North 20th Ward.

In January, 1944, he went to Oak Ridge, Tennessee, as an engineer for the Manhatten Atomic Energy Project, and while there, until 1946, he was president of the local branch of the Church.

Back in Salt Lake City again, he was sustained Patriarch to the Church on April 6, 1947, and since that time he has traveled throughout the stakes of the Church as one of the General Authorities. He has given over thirteen thousand patriarchal blessings.

He married Jeanne Ness August 17, 1932, in the Salt Lake Temple. They have two sons, three daughters, and twelve grandchildren.

ELDRED G. SMITH

"What a Patriarchal Blessing Can Do"

An example of what a patriarchal blessing can do came to me in a story which I have repeated many times, which a woman told me. As a young woman she lived in a small town. When she finished high school, there was no further opportunity to continue her education. There was no further opportunity to get work so that she could be independent, so she came to Salt Lake City where she found herself a job. As time came for registration at the University, she became very anxious to go to school again, and knowing that there was not a possibility, under present conditions, she felt quite disheartened. She went to the patriarch and received her patriarchal blessing, and in the blessing he promised her that she should receive a good education. She was elated, and she went out of the office feeling very happy. Before she had gone half a block, she said, she fell to earth out of her cloud with a realization that going to college cost money, and she did not have any, nor the means to get it. The opportunity and possibility of going to college at present did not seem to be at all possible, which made her very downhearted again. And the thought came to her to go visit her aunt, who was living in

Salt Lake City. Without stopping to analyze that impression she turned, and instead of going back to work she went to visit her aunt and told her aunt of her experience—cried on her shoulder. And her aunt said to her, "I know an elderly woman who lives down the street a few blocks. She has at various times helped young girls get through college in return for the help the girls can give to her. I do not know whether she has help now or not, but," she said, "this woman knows who I am. Go down and see her and tell her I sent you."

She went on the run to this elderly woman's home, and within two weeks from the time she received her patriarchal blessing, she registered at the University of Utah, signed a promissory note to pay for her education, and eventually paid for it. She said if she had stopped to question the first impression she got to go visit her aunt, she would have said to herself, "Why should I go visit my aunt and tell her my troubles? I came to Salt Lake City to be independent; why not be independent? She cannot help me with my troubles; she has enough of her own. She doesn't have space in her home to let me sleep there, let alone board me or help me. Why need I go and bother my aunt?" But she did not stop to analyze that impression; she acted on it. As a result she met the woman who gave her the opportunity of receiving her education.

(*Conference Report*, April 1952, pp. 39-40.)

ELDRED G. SMITH

"I Met the Challenge"

Live the gospel first, then teach it to others. Declare your testimony to others on every occasion. There is a power in bearing your testimony.

I remember an occasion in the mission field in Germany, when I had been tracting. I was getting a bit discouraged, having met nothing but passive attention. After climbing some stairs I knocked on a door, and a large man opened it and with a very gruff attitude greeted me. I gave him my brief message, as we did in those days in presenting a tract at the door. He turned and picked up a handful of leaflets off the table near the door, and shook them in my face, and declared to me that I was the fifth person who had been to his door that day with just such leaflets. He was a large man and very rough in his approach. I expected any moment that I might be thrown down the stairs, but he declared that none of us knew that we had the gospel. He said, "You all say that it is true, this is the way; you all say that. None of you know."

I met the challenge, and I stood straight before him and looked him square in the eyes. And I bore my testimony to him that I knew that this is the gospel of Jesus Christ and the only method by which he could gain salvation, and I went on at some length bearing my testimony to this man. Afterward I was surprised at the fluency of my speech because I had not been in Germany very long. I did not understand the language very well, but when I had finished, he had changed his tone entirely and very humbly begged my pardon and promised to read the tract, which I am sure he did.

(*Conference Report*, October 1951, pp. 81-82.)

ELDRED G. SMITH

"I Am Healed, I Am Well"

Just recently a woman told me of her experience. She became very ill. It had been determined that she had cancer. She had gone through surgery on numerous occasions, until she had come to a point where the doctors had given her up and told her that she did not have months to live, but only weeks. There was no hope for her. She was living at home with a nurse to take care of her. A neighbor called one day. She had a phone near her bed so she could answer it, and the neighbor said to her, "Now when the doorbell rings, don't answer it. It is just those Mormon missionaries coming down the street; so when the doorbell rings, just don't answer it. Don't pay any attention to it."

So the woman thanked her for her consideration, her kindness. She told her nurse that when the doorbell rang she was not to answer it; it was just those Mormon missionaries and to pay no attention to them. Well, the doorbell rang after a few minutes, and the nurse, from force of habit, opened the door, then realized that she had been told not to. She quickly disposed of the missionaries. Immediately after, the nurse left the house to get some groceries. There came a knock on the door. For some reason or other the missionaries had returned. They knocked and got no answer, so they opened the door and called in. Hearing a response from an inner room they went on in. The woman said the missionaries came and stood beside her bed and mumbled a little between themselves, something she did not understand. Then one of them said, "Well, it's highly irregular, but I guess if you say so it is all right." The next thing she knew she had been administered to by these Mormon missionaries.

She said when they took their hands off her head she sat

up in bed. She got out of bed and went into the kitchen and got some food from her refrigerator. Then she excused herself while she dressed. The missionaries made an appointment to come back at another time. When the nurse returned and saw the woman was up and around, she told her to get back into bed. "No, I'm not going back to bed. I am healed. I am well," the woman said.

The nurse, thinking she was delirious, called the doctor. The doctor also ordered her to get back into bed, but she refused again and said she was well. Over a year later, after the doctor had told her she had but weeks to live, she came to Salt Lake City and went to the temple, then came to my office for a blessing. She was very happy, thrilled as she had never been before in her life. The happiest part of her life has been since the doctor told her she couldn't live. Yet she said it was not the experience of healing alone that gave her a testimony of the gospel.

(Eldred G. Smith, "That Ye May Know the Truth," *Improvement Era*, 62:940.)

ELDRED G. SMITH

"Why Should We Question the Resurrection?"

It was mentioned that I did some work in Oak Ridge, Tennessee, in engineering. I think one of the experiences I had there taught me or brought to mind a firm and rigid demonstration of one of the sound principles of the gospel. I remember in engineering work we had to go into a private, small classroom with a sloped floor and benches, with an oak table and a blackboard at one end. With about twenty-five of us in the room, they closed the door and put a guard at the outside to see that nobody listened through the keyhole. Then they would give us instructions on the development of the process of the atomic energy work there.

I remember on a number of occasions the head scientist or physicist who came to talk to us would pound that oak table with his fist to emphasize the fact that nothing can be destroyed. The Prophet Joseph Smith told us that a long time ago, and we have it recorded in the Doctrine and Covenants that the elements of the earth are eternal. (D&C 93:33.)

To me this is a very sound principle because it follows through various other principles of the gospel, without which there would be no resurrection, and many other things would have to be different than they are now.

They proved that in their work in Oak Ridge. I remember on one occasion, as I was doing some checking around the plant, there was a group of men gathered. I inquired as to what was going on. There was a little excitement there. There was a group of men gathered around a wooden box about a cubic yard in size. They broke this box open and it was full of hacksaw blades. I was told that in the process, from one stage to another, they were losing inventory. They knew they could not lose inventory of the element they were working with, which was uranium, of course.

So this crew of men came in with their hacksaws and cut out all the piping between one stage and the other in the process—cut these pipes into short lengths, cut them open lengthwise, put them through a chemical recovery process, and brought their inventory up to where it was supposed to have been, because the elements had been coating the inside walls of the pipe. They knew it had to be somewhere, and they had traced down all other sources, so that by process of elimination, I suppose, they found that it had to be within those pipes. So they went to the expense of tearing out the pipes and building it up again.

They had a beautiful floor-scrubbing machine. I think Brother Bishop will remember this one. I was just talking to him a few minutes ago. The floors in the production buildings there were a smooth concrete, not painted, because they were constantly scrubbed with this beautiful chrome floor-scrubbing machine. This machine could carry its own supply of water and soap and was electrically operated. They would just push it along, and it would scrub the floor and gather up everything and dry it as it went along, all in one process. All that the machine gathered up, and the machine itself was put into an acid bath and a chemical recovery process so that if in moving the units around, there was any of the material that ever got on the floor, they would be able to gather it up and recover it. Even though it might be a very small, minute particle, it was still recoverable, and they had to recover it in order to keep their inventory up because they knew it could not be destroyed. There were several other demonstrations that I saw of that same principle.

If this principle is true—and we know it is—then why should we question the resurrection, for instance? Even though this body goes into the grave and is decomposed, or if it is burned or if it is lost at sea—no matter what is done to this body after death—the elements of this body are elements of the earth and cannot be destroyed. We have learned through this process of smashing the atom, and so forth, that we can break up the particles of the elements of the earth. We have learned some principles of restoring them again. A simple example is that of water. If you heat it, it goes to steam. If you keep it under control and condense it and cool it, you bring it back to water again.

I believe that is true of all the elements of the earth. We can break them down, and if we knew the law and had the power to put the law into operation, we could reunite them again and restore them as they were.

(*Speeches of the Year,* "Exaltation," March 10, 1964, pp. 2-3.)

ELDRED G. SMITH

"The Only Ones Sitting in the Audience"

I have heard President Clark a number of times refer to his theme song, as he calls it, that of unity; and with his permission I would like to join his chorus. We should all join his chorus, not only in words, but in action. Paul taught the same doctrine when he wrote to the Ephesians:

"I therefore . . . beseech you that ye walk worthy of the vocation wherewith ye are called,

"With all lowliness and meekness, with longsuffering, forbearing one another in love;

"Endeavoring to keep the unity of the Spirit in the bond of peace.

"There is one body, and one Spirit, even as ye are called in one hope of your calling;

"One Lord, one faith, one baptism,

"One God and Father of all, who is above all, and through all, and in you all." (Eph. 4:1-6.)

When I talk about unity in the gospel, I am often reminded of an experience that I had while on a mission in Germany. When this German choir sang to us yesterday in the conference meetings, I was reminded again of those experiences, especially when I was assigned to work in Celle in the Hannover District in Germany. Once a month we went to the little town of Uelzen, which was a self-sustaining branch. We went there to get their reports and to help them as we could. My companion was assigned to the branch the same time I was, so this first visit to Uelzen was a new experience for both of us.

We took our seats in the first meeting we attended in the front of the hall. The branch president announced that the meeting would be started by the choir singing such and such a song. I looked about and found no choir up in front, but before

I could ask any questions or discover an answer to the problem in my mind as to where the choir was coming from, my companion and I found ourselves the only ones sitting in the audience. The entire congregation, except for my companion and I, had gone up to the front and sang as a choir. It is no wonder we have Saints who can come here and produce a chorus such as we had yesterday.

I found from the reports that they not only all sang together, but they worked together. I found that there was 100 percent membership of the branch paying 100 percent tithing—and that was not just the month that I went there on that one visit, but that was the report I got all the time I was there. Attendance in their meetings was the same. They worked together in everything they did. I discovered also that there were two women in the branch at that time whose husbands had gone to America, and that the branch had agreed together, before these two men left, that they would all work together. They would keep the commandments of the Lord to the best of their ability; they would do all that was required of them without excuse; nothing would stop them from fulfilling the responsibilities given to them. Those who remained in the branch would see to it that the wives of these two men were taken care of, that they would not be in need.

The two men who left for America agreed that they would do likewise in living the commandments of the Lord, and that they would find jobs and work hard and save their money and send for their wives as soon as possible. It was not long until I was transferred from that section of Germany, and then soon after, I was released to come home.

Some twenty years later, after I became the Patriarch to the Church, I had an appointment to give a blessing to a young girl. When she arrived, her mother was with her. I found that the mother was one of those two sisters whose husbands had left Uelzen when I was over there. I had a long talk with this sister and her daughter. The daughter, of course, had grown up from a small child, and her mother told me this story: that one by one, or two at a time, as occasion came, different members of the branch would have the opportunity of leaving and coming to America, until finally, before World War II broke out, there was not one member of the Church left in that branch in Uelzen. They had all come to America safely before the war broke out.

Then she told me also that in the end of the war, when the American soldiers invaded that section of Germany, for some reason unknown to her, the German soldiers set up a resistance in Uelzen which resulted in a four-day battle. The bombings and general destruction were such that there was not a house left in the section where most of the Saints had lived, yet there was not a member of the Church left in Uelzen —a result and reward of unity, working together to keep the commandments of the Lord.

This is a challenge to us, brothers and sisters, that we might do as they did in Uelzen—that we might live the commandments of the Lord as they did.

(*Conference Report*, October 1955, pp. 62-63.)

ELDRED G. SMITH

"This Is Priesthood Order"

In the beginning, God said: "It is not good for man to be alone."

One of the fundamental purposes of this life is to have experiences whereby we may learn to be perfect. Man is not perfect without the woman, nor is the woman perfect without the man.

Priesthood and motherhood go hand in hand. Neither is

complete without the other. Both are eternal. A perfect family requires the proper fulfillment of both. This life is to help us fulfill these two responsibilities, that we may exercise them through eternity.

Priesthood is patriarchal, which means "of the fathers." A married man is the patriarch of his home and is responsible to bless members of his family. The exercising of this privilege could be a means of preventing many broken homes. We think of a priesthood holder as one who should bless his children, baptize and confirm them, and perform the other ordinances of the gospel in behalf of members of his family. His responsibility is not only to bless his children, but his wife is an important member of his family too. Yes, we think of blessing the wife when she is sick, but if the relationship between husband and wife becomes a bit strained, wouldn't it be a good thing for the husband to give his wife a blessing for the purpose of increasing the unity and love for each other?

I remember an experience I had when a good sister who wanted a special blessing came to my office. When I asked her why she wanted a special blessing, she refused to tell me. I learned from her that her husband was a member of the Church and held the Melchizedek Priesthood, so I spent considerable time trying to teach her the principle of priesthood order, where the father in the home should bless the members of the family, and concluded a long discussion of teaching her this principle by having her go home to get her blessing from her husband instead of from me.

Sometime later she returned to my office, refreshed my memory of this experience, and said she left my office very resentful. Here I thought I had done a good job in teaching her this principle of priesthood order, so I had to ask more questions to find out what had happened.

She said the reason she refused to tell me why she wanted a blessing was that she wanted the blessing because there wasn't the proper relationship between her and her husband, and then I had sent her home to get a blessing from her husband. So naturally she was a little bit resentful.

Then she added, "That was one of the finest things that

ever happened." She said she went home, she prayed about it, she thought about it, and then finally she mustered enough courage to ask her husband for the blessing. Of course it shocked him, but she was patient; she let him think it over a bit, ponder about it, and pray about it; and finally he gave her a blessing. Then she added, "There has never been such a fine relationship in our home in all our lives as we have had since he gave me that blessing."

I could see what had happened. This is a two-way street. First, she had to clean her side of the slate and humble herself. Then she asked him for the blessing, and he had to humble himself and clean his side of the slate. Then he sealed the blessing upon her which they had fulfilled by living the law upon which the blessing was predicated. This is priesthood order.

(*Conference Report*, April 1965, pp. 114-15.)

ELDRED G. SMITH

"He Had Quit Several Times"

Humility is one of the qualities that helps build faith. Would a missionary be successful if he were not humble? He has to be teachable, with a receptive mind, before he can teach others. And to be teachable, he must be humble. And we should all be missionaries.

All the requirements of living the gospel become easier through humility.

A young man told me his experience in becoming a member of the Church, which is typical of many in their activities of investigating the Church. He said the missionaries came to the lesson on the Word of Wisdom. He and his wife were both users of tobacco. After the meeting was over and the missionaries had left, they talked it over with each other and decided among themselves, "Well, if that is what the Lord wants and if this is the Lord's Church, we will try it." He said that he was not particularly concerned about himself, he thought he could do it easily. He was worried about his wife; she had never tried to quit before. On the other hand, he had quit several times. After proving to himself that he could quit, of course, he went back to the use of cigarettes again. But he said in this case it was just the reverse.

His wife quit without any apparent difficulty, but he had tremendous difficulty. He became nervous and irritable. He could not rest. He was cranky among his fellow workers. He could not sleep at night. But inasmuch as his wife had quit, he was not going to be outdone by her. So, one night, he became so restless, so disturbed that he could not sleep, and his wife suggested to him that he pray about it. He thought that was a good joke. He ridiculed the idea of prayer; he said, "This is something I have to do. Nobody can help me with this. I can do this." But as the night passed and he had done everything he could to stimulate sleep and rest without any success, finally in despair, he humbled himself enough to kneel at the side of the bed and pray vocally.

According to his own testimony, he said that he got up from his prayer, got into bed, went to sleep, and has never been tempted by cigarettes since. He has absolutely lost his taste for tobacco. He said, "The Word of Wisdom was not a health program for me. It was a lesson of humility." He said, "I had to learn humility." That is what it meant to him. As it is with many of the requirements of the Church, we have to demonstrate humble obedience.

(*Conference Report*, April 1955, p. 42.)

ELDRED G. SMITH

"How Did You Know?"

People say, "Well, how do you declare lineage? . . ."

I had another occasion I originally had in mind to tell. Brother Wallace Toronto (many of you probably know the Toronto family)—Wallace Toronto was the mission president in Czechoslovakia. When that mission was closed he turned that mission over to another couple and returned home. Later he brought this couple into my office for a blessing. They came into Canada and then into the United States. Wallace Toronto and I went to high school together, so we started reminiscing old days a little.

In the middle of our discussion of reminiscing, I turned to the lady of this couple and said, "Would you be surprised if you had Jewish blood in your line? You have, don't you?"

She said, "How did you know?"

Wallace Toronto's face dropped about so long, his mouth dropped open, and he said, "Why, Eldred, I've known these people for years, and it has never dawned on me that there was Jewish mixture in her line. How did you know?"

I said, "Well, if you had asked me out on the street I couldn't have told you. There's not any Jewish mixture in your husband's line, is there—just in yours?" I asked her, and they confirmed it as being correct.

I could tell you three or four very similar experiences, definite experiences I have had where it has just come to me that there was a mixture of certain lineage in an individual and I stated it to them before they told me.

(University of Utah Forum Address, January 17, 1964, pp. 12-13.)

236

ELDRED G. SMITH

"Bishop, I See What You Came Here to Tell Me"

I am reminded of the story which is so often told, and which you all know, of the bishop who visited a member who had become inactive in the ward. They sat in front of an open fire in the fireplace in silence. And the bishop, presumably thinking about how he could approach the subject, reached forth with the tongs and lifted a hot, live coal from the fire and set it on the hearth in front of the fire. They sat in silence and watched the hot, live coal gradually turn cold and black and lifeless. Then the bishop picked up the coal again with the tongs, and set it back into the fire with the other living coals, and watched it again regain its life and its fire and its heat and its warmth. Still nothing was said. Finally the man said, "Bishop, I see what you came here to tell me."

Through meeting together the fire of our testimony is kept alive and glowing. It is through meeting and working together that we grow in faith and in knowledge. When we withdraw from Church activity we become as the lone coal on the hearth, cold and lifeless.

(*Conference Report*, April 1953, p. 29.)

Biographical Sketch

BISHOP JOHN H. VANDENBERG

Bishop John H. Vandenberg is the Presiding Bishop of The Church of Jesus Christ of Latter-day Saints, the ninth since the Church was organized in 1830.

His duties include membership on the Church Expenditures Committee, the General Priesthood Committee, and the Church Correlation Committee. Since May 1963, he has been chairman of the General Church Welfare Committee. He presides over the Aaronic Priesthood and is chairman of the General Scouting Committee and the Health Services Corporation of the Church.

Bishop Vandenberg has been closely associated with the vast building program of the Church since 1955, having served as vice-chairman of the Building Committee in charge of finances.

His previous Church experiences include a mission to the Netherlands as a young man in 1925-1928, where he served as mission secretary. He has been a stake mission president, first counselor in the Denver Stake presidency, and second counselor in the Ensign (Salt Lake City) Stake presidency, from which position he was called to be Presiding Bishop of the Church in October 1961.

Bishop Vandenberg was formerly engaged in the merchandising of wool and livestock in Denver. He was also associated in textile manufacturing and ranching in that city.

Bishop Vandenberg was born in 1904 in Ogden, Utah, where he received his formal education. He is married to the former Ariena Stok, and they have two married daughters, Mrs. Lenore V. Mendenhall and Mrs. Norine V. Francis, both of Salt Lake City, Utah.

JOHN H. VANDENBERG

"Following Counsel"

$\mathbf{A}$ few years ago, a bishop from a small agricultural town visited my office to arrange for the dedication of the meetinghouse in his ward. During our conversation he told me that when he was advised by the Brethren to build a meetinghouse, he had many doubts, since it was a small community with modest resources. He said, "I didn't have the slightest idea where the money was coming from, but following counsel, we started; and the funds came, and now we are ready to dedicate, having all bills paid." Then he added, "And do you know, the tithing paid by those good Saints has increased over 600 percent during the three-year period!" I have never seen a person filled with more joy and satisfaction than this good bishop, who simply followed counsel.

(Conference Report, October 1964, p. 41.)

241

JOHN H. VANDENBERG

"Thanks for the Lesson"

You know you can get great experiences with money. I recall that when I came home from my mission my first objective was to get a job. My parents and I apparently didn't think that it was necessary to go to college in those days.

Jobs were scarce. It was the beginning of the depression, and I asked my father, "Where can I get a job?"

He said, "I don't know; I will keep my ears open."

He was in the bishopric. At a bishop's meeting they had a committee meeting; and one of the men came in there, and my dad asked, "Do any of you know where my son can get a job?"

The one fellow said, "Yes, I happened to hear that a feed yard out in West Ogden needs a bookkeeper."

My father gave me that information, and I went out there, and I got the job. I walked four miles to get it.

When I got there, the man said, "Can you keep books?"

I said, "I think so."

He said, "Go to work. At the end of the day I will let you know whether you are any good or not." At the end of the day, he said, "You are all right. Come back in the morning."

In the morning I got up early and walked another four miles. In the evening I walked back four miles. That was a little monotonous, so I enticed my brother to drive me out there for about a week. That was all right, but this put him way out of his way, so I thought, "Well, I guess I had better buy myself a car."

I went to the used-car lot, and I saw an old jitney there. The side windows were broken. There were no floor boards in it.

I said, "Does it run?"

He said, "Yes, it runs."

I said, "How much?"

He said, "$100.00."

I said, "I'll take it."

He said, "That's fine. That's $100.00, cash."

I said, "I don't have cash."

He said, "You go to a financial institution and borrow the money, and you come here with the cash, because we don't loan money."

I went to the financial institution. I said, "I would like to borrow $100.00."

He rubbed his hands, and he said, "What do you want the $100.00 for?"

I said, "I need to buy a car."

So he pulled out some papers, and he said, "You sign here and then you go home and get your father to sign the other line." Lots of fine print.

I took it home and I said, "Dad, I need a car. The only way I can get one is to buy one, and I can borrow $100.00. I've got one that I've spotted that runs."

He said, "Okay, $100.00 doesn't look like a lot of money." He didn't read the fine print, neither did I.

I went to the institution; I got my $100.00. I gave it to the used car man, and I got my car. It served quite well. Every month a notice came from the institution for me to pay so much, and I paid it. At the end of the six months, the paid note came back. I had paid my obligation. Casually I sat down and figured out how much I had paid. On that $100.00, I had repaid $140.00!

I went to the man at the institution, and I said, "Sir, you've made a mistake."

He said, "What do you mean?"

I said, "I borrowed $100.00, and I gave you back $140.00. Something is wrong."

He said, "There is nothing wrong. This is service charges and interest."

I said, "You mean 40 percent in six months, which is 80 percent annually!"

He said, "That's right."

I said, "Thanks for the lesson." That was the best lesson I ever had. I learned the power of interest, and I used that power for my own benefit after that. I never bought anything unless I could pay for it. Take care of money. Watch your money and spend it wisely, and don't buy anything that you can't take care of.

(*Speeches of the Year,* "What Will You Choose," February 28, 1967, pp. 8-11.)

JOHN H. VANDENBERG

"The True Fiber"

Life has many parallels. I remember . . . as I was married and got a job, I went to work for a very energetic young man from Chicago who had moved out to Ogden. We were in the sheep business; we were sheep merchants. We were quite successful, and like all successful businesses, we thought we would want to expand. We saw in the West a vast number of sheep here, and we saw the wool coming off these sheep. So we decided that we wanted to get into the wool business, which was related to the industry that we were in.

True, we didn't know much about the wool business—all the experts were back east in the Boston area and in the New England states. When these wool buyers would come out from the eastern states, they would go up to a grower, and they would take a look at his wool as it came off the sheep's back. They were usually there at the shearing corral. The shearer would tie the fleece and would hand it to the wool buyer. The wool buyer would look at it and would take out a strand or two, pulled from the fleece, to see what the staple was. Then he would look at the color to see how much dirt there was in it, the grease content; were there any burrs in it, any chaff? Then, in his mind he would calculate that the price in Boston for clean wool might be one dollar per pound, and would say to himself, "This fleece shrinks 55 percent. All I am interested in is, what is the pure content of this fleece in wool, when it comes to the pure fiber content of the thing that I have in my hands?"

He would be thinking of this wool as it whipped through the scouring plant where all the residue is extracted—the grease taken out—and as it came through the top manufacturing machines where it would become a strand of pure white wool. This was all that mattered to him, and he would try to analyze the fleece as best he could. The only way that he could analyze it was from previous experience of working at purchased wool. He had estimated what the wool would shrink, and then it went back to Boston through the mills. And they would send him a report of how accurately he had estimated. Well, it doesn't take very long, I assume, when a man makes 100 purchases, that he finds out where his mistakes have been, to where he adjusts in his observation and then comes up with a pretty close answer. Well, we had to go through all of this.

The thing that I learned from that business, although we were quite successful in it, was that there was a parallel there—that in this simple fleece of wool the only thing that counted was the true fiber, the pure wool. This was like life. The only thing that counts in life is the pure moral fiber that is within each of us—that after all is said and all is done with life, when we come to the end, what is our life but what we have made of it that is worthwhile?

(*Speeches of the Year*, "What Will You Choose," February 28, 1967, pp. 3-4.)

J O H N   H.   V A N D E N B E R G

"The Most Wonderful Thing in the World"

Learning comes pretty early in life. I remember as a lad, when I was about twelve years old, I was walking down the street with a friend who was not a member of the Church. This was during World War I. We heard a racket overhead. We looked and there was a biplane—a little cloth plane making a terrible racket. We looked up and admired and marveled at what was going on.

I said to my companion, "Isn't it wonderful?"

My companion said, "The most wonderful thing in the world!"

As he said that, I stopped and thought for a moment—I don't know why a twelve-year-old boy would think. Then I said, "No, friend, that is *not* the most important thing in the world. *True religion* is the most important thing in the world."

I suppose I had said that because of the training that I had had in Sunday School and in Primary and in my home, because I come from a home where my parents were good Latter-day Saints. And they were very desirous that their children learn of the true gospel. I suppose from birth, and being in this environment, it started to sink in.

To know that true religion is the most important thing in life, I think, has played a very important part in my life.

(*Speeches of the Year*, "What Will You Choose," February 28, 1967, pp. 2-3.)

JOHN H. VANDENBERG

"Now You Can Get Further Behind"

Just as He organized His church in His day, conferring His authority upon His brethren, commanding them to pursue the salvation of mankind, so has He in these latter days restored His church, and revealed His priesthood, and commissioned those who receive the priesthood to warn, expound, exhort, teach, and invite all to come unto Christ. Then, as members do come into His Church, He also commissions His priesthood to visit the house of each member, exhorting them to pray vocally and in secret and to attend to all family duties. For this is the only way to keep His kingdom strong. His charge to us is to be with and strengthen our brethren.

To those who diligently pursue such a course, miracles come to pass, evidenced by testimonies that declare: "He was dead, and is alive again; he was lost, and is found."

So wrote one sister. She, having been born and raised in another church, states that she and her Mormon husband lived the first years of their marriage without any religious activity. One evening two pleasant fellows appeared at their door and introduced themselves as home teachers. With little encouragement, they kept coming, month after month. Then the husband began, for the first time, to read such Church books as he had.

The sister said that when they moved to another town she packed the books away where she hoped her husband would never find them again. Sure enough, the couple again forgot about religion until other home teachers arrived at their new home.

After the first visit of these new teachers, her husband searched for his books until he found them. The sister states

247

that the one teacher was so friendly that they couldn't help liking him, and when he began inviting them to Church affairs, they accepted because he seemed to really want them there and they didn't want to disappoint him.

"Finally," said the sister, "after calling for many months, he asked if he could offer a prayer in our home, and we didn't know how to refuse. So the first prayer ever offered in our home was by this home teacher.

"About this time our teenage son began to complain at being sent to my church while neither his father nor I was attending church ourselves. So we compromised by attending the Mormon Church and my church on alternate Sundays.

"Our home teachers had been calling on us for about two years when they asked if the missionaries might call. (We had had them in our former town, but I had refused to listen to them.) This time I agreed to hear the missionaries, but failed to make any effort to listen or understand, and refused to read any of the material that was given to me. After the fourth call, the missionaries handed me more pamphlets and suggested that I read fifty more pages in the Book of Mormon (I had read none of the book yet); then one of them said good-naturedly, 'Now you can get further behind.'

"Suddenly I was ashamed of my attitude and determined to read the entire Book of Mormon before his next visit. I carried out this promise, and when the missionaries returned I told them I wanted to be baptized. As a result of these efforts by the priesthood brethren, the family was unified and is now enjoying the true purpose of life in harmony with the principles and teachings of the gospel.

(*Conference Report*, October 1970, p. 11.)

JOHN H. VANDENBERG

"My Father Works There"

The story is told of a teacher who was quizzing her students about the products being manufactured in a nearby building. "Who can tell me what is manufactured in that plant?" she inquired, pointing toward the factory visible from the classroom window.

Quickly a small lad raised his hand and named a number of products. The teacher, amazed at his answer, said, "That is correct, but how did you know?"

"That's easy," replied the boy. "My father works there, and that's what he brings home in his lunch pail every night."

This may seem humorous, but it carries serious consequences; for the boy had unwittingly disclosed the dishonest act of his father, and by its repetition had already erroneously been taught by example that such an act was all right.

(*Conference Report*, April 1967, p. 15.)

JOHN H. VANDENBERG

"Home Plate Doesn't Move"

I am thinking right now of an interview held once with Satchel Page. He was a great baseball player—a great pitcher. And someone came up and said, "Satchel, what's your secret?"

"Well," he said, "you know, I take that ball and I throw it right over home plate. That's what I try to do every time. You know, home plate doesn't move."

And in his philosophy he knows and has recognized that there is one thing to do, and that is always to live according to the law.

(*Speeches of the Year*, "Be Leaders with Spiritual Wisdom and Stability," March 4, 1969, p. 7.)

JOHN H. VANDENBERG

"I Guess You'll Have to Walk"

My wife and I were married during the time of the depression. I had purchased a new car, and it was all paid for. I was employed; my salary was $125 per month. I remember bringing home my first check. My wife said, "It isn't very much, is it?" I replied, "No, but it will do." She said, "Yes, if we budget it." So we sat down and budgeted: $12.50 for tithing; $1.00 for fast offerings; $45 for rent; $40 for food, and additional amounts for utilities and clothing; and $10 in the savings account, for we presumed and anticipated that a child would come eventually. When we added it all up, the $125 was all allocated. I said to my wife, "It's all gone, and there isn't any left to buy gasoline for my car. What am I going to do?" She replied, "Sorry. I guess you'll have to walk."

So I walked back and forth to work. And the car stayed right in the garage for several months until I got a raise and could spare a little to buy gasoline. We've always managed to get along on my income, and I don't think we have ever had an unhappy moment over it, but rather, much satisfaction in coping with the situation. It isn't so much what you earn, but how you manage.

(*Conference Report*, September 1967, p. 78.)

JOHN H. VANDENBERG

"My Dearest Father Bishopric"

Sometime ago a letter came to my desk, written by a woman investigator, which carried with it a great deal of enthusiasm and testimony, and I would like to share with you tonight the following excerpts from this letter. Her salutation was this:

My dearest Father Bishopric:

You are going to be rather surprised to hear from me, but I attended Sunday services of The Church of Jesus Christ of Latter-day Saints today and was so inspired. . . .

I owe my gratitude to just about the finest, well-cultured, and intellectual gentlemen. . . . They graciously invited themselves into my home and explained the Mormons. . . . I just had to go to church with them on the following Sunday. The book on how Joseph Smith tells his own story was so outstanding, with great love of God for each and every human being, that my knowledge of religion certainly broadened just by meeting these two elders. . . .

On entering the church I was so astonished to see how many young people of today are attending church, and especially thrilled to see how the young mothers bring their lovely children. . . . The thing that touched me deeply is how the elders or brothers were so anxious just to be able to say, "How do you do". . . . This is something you don't see in other churches. . . .

The Aaronic Priesthood conducted the sacrament . . . which was so pure with delight, followed by the separation to classes. At this time the elders led me to the adult class. . . . Here is where I accumulated knowledge in one half hour that I did not know in a lifetime of fifty years. . . .

I also enjoyed the opening prayer . . . which put a dent in my mind that these are a group of people that have to be made more known in our United States of America. . . .

Again I say how happy I was to attend services in your Mormon Latter-day Saint Church, and how mighty proud the mission must be of the elders. They are an inspiration that many mothers and fathers today can learn the message from God to his children to make this a better world to live in like God intended it to be.

As I read this thrilling letter, I thought, what a great blessing to the elder's parents and to those missionaries, although they are unaware of the great spiritual lift that they gave to this woman. As the woman stated, "I owe my gratitude to just about the finest, well-cultured, and intellectual gentlemen." I wondered what greater honor could there be than to be so highly esteemed by one's neighbors. No doubt this experience is happening time and time again the world over.

(*Conference Report,* April 1962, p. 84.)

JOHN H. VANDENBERG

"We Now Have Two Healthy Lambs"

Just the other day I received a written testimony from a mother expressing appreciation for a servant of the Lord. This servant, a home teacher, was simply following the Lord's assignment to "watch over the church always, and be with and strengthen them." (D&C 20:53.) She writes:

John H. Vandenberg

"My husband had taken some Scouts to the Merit Badge Pow-Wow at BYU. It was a two-hundred mile drive so they had left at 4 o'clock in the morning. When I awakened, my main concern was for their safety, as it was snowing and blowing. My eight-year-old boy had already awakened and left on his bicycle for the corral, about a mile away, to do the chores. Suddenly there he was in the bedroom with a big tear in each eye.

" 'Mama, we've got two little lambs out to the farm and they are wet and shaking, and I tried to call you from the service station but you had to have a dime, so I just wrapped my coat around them and rode home as fast as I could.'

"My husband had acquired a small herd of ewes only last fall as a father-son project, but my son and I were completely inexperienced in the process of 'lambing.' I knew that we had to have help from someone. Whom could we call? I don't recall which one of us thought of it first, but suddenly both of us knew it would be our home teacher.

"Within twenty minutes he was at the corral with his eight-year-old boy and mine. He stayed for three hours, working with the lambs every minute. The sheep had not been sheared, as the expected lambing date was still a month away, but he understood and did those things which needed to be done. One lamb looked quite strong, but there was not much hope for the second. Just before dinner he returned to the house with one of the lambs in a box. Would I try to get it warm? He was taking the other one to his home to work with it. He would be back within two hours to take them both back to their mother for nursing.

"I am certain that he spent over six hours that Saturday at our farm working with our sheep and our boy. As a result we now have two healthy lambs and an even more beloved home teacher. I cannot tell you how much our eight-year-old boy thinks of the home teacher who worked side by side with him through one entire day teaching by example the love that is our gospel."

(*Conference Report*, April 1968, pp. 46-47.)

TOPICAL INDEX

Listed according to author followed by page number.

Abbreviations:

Achievement

VLB - - - - - - - - - - - - - - - - - 43
PHD - - - - - - - - - - - - - - - - - 101
MJA - - - - - - - - - - - - - - - - - 13
VLB - - - - - - - - - - - - - - - - - 46
MC - - - - - - - - - - - - - - - - - 63

Brotherly Love

MJA - - - - - - - - - - - - - - - - - 14
ETB - - - - - - - - - - - - - - - - - 31
MC - - - - - - - - - - - - - - - - - 64
MC - - - - - - - - - - - - - - - - - 69
MC - - - - - - - - - - - - - - - - - 71
PHD - - - - - - - - - - - - - - - - - 110
HRJ - - - - - - - - - - - - - - - - - 194
RLS - - - - - - - - - - - - - - - - - 216
JHV - - - - - - - - - - - - - - - - - 252
SWK - - - - - - - - - - - - - - - - - 156

Compassion

ETB - - - - - - - - - - - - - - - - - 34
MC - - - - - - - - - - - - - - - - - 67
MC - - - - - - - - - - - - - - - - - 70
LCD - - - - - - - - - - - - - - - - - 90
LCD - - - - - - - - - - - - - - - - - 96
RLS - - - - - - - - - - - - - - - - - 215
RLS - - - - - - - - - - - - - - - - - 216
SWK - - - - - - - - - - - - - - - - - 156

Conversion

VLB - - - - - - - - - - - - - - - - - 49
MC - - - - - - - - - - - - - - - - - 69

HRJ - - - - - - - - - - - - - - - - - 188
EGS - - - - - - - - - - - - - - - - - 226
JHV - - - - - - - - - - - - - - - - - 247

Courage

VLB - - - - - - - - - - - - - - - - - 43
PHD - - - - - - - - - - - - - - - - - 105
PHD - - - - - - - - - - - - - - - - - 107
PHD - - - - - - - - - - - - - - - - - 116
ARD - - - - - - - - - - - - - - - - - 141
HRJ - - - - - - - - - - - - - - - - - 191
JHV - - - - - - - - - - - - - - - - - 244
MEP - - - - - - - - - - - - - - - - - 172
SWK - - - - - - - - - - - - - - - - - 150
SWK - - - - - - - - - - - - - - - - - 151
EGS - - - - - - - - - - - - - - - - - 225

Dedication

MJA - - - - - - - - - - - - - - - - - 13
ETB - - - - - - - - - - - - - - - - - 23
ETB - - - - - - - - - - - - - - - - - 24
ETB - - - - - - - - - - - - - - - - - 29
VLB - - - - - - - - - - - - - - - - - 46
VLB - - - - - - - - - - - - - - - - - 49
MC - - - - - - - - - - - - - - - - - 61
MC - - - - - - - - - - - - - - - - - 73
PHD - - - - - - - - - - - - - - - - - 107
PHD - - - - - - - - - - - - - - - - - 116
PHD - - - - - - - - - - - - - - - - - 120
PHD - - - - - - - - - - - - - - - - - 122
JHV - - - - - - - - - - - - - - - - - 250
SWK - - - - - - - - - - - - - - - - - 153

Duty

MJA - - - - - - - - - - - - - - - - - - - 16
MC - - - - - - - - - - - - - - - - - - - 72
PHD - - - - - - - - - - - - - - - - - - - 110
MJA - - - - - - - - - - - - - - - - - - - 13
VLB - - - - - - - - - - - - - - - - - - - 49
SWK - - - - - - - - - - - - - - - - - - - 149

Example

MJA - - - - - - - - - - - - - - - - - - - 14
PHD - - - - - - - - - - - - - - - - - - - 101
MEP - - - - - - - - - - - - - - - - - - - 166
MPE - - - - - - - - - - - - - - - - - - - 173
SWK - - - - - - - - - - - - - - - - - - - 150

Faith

VLB - - - - - - - - - - - - - - - - - - - 46
VLB - - - - - - - - - - - - - - - - - - - 49
MC - - - - - - - - - - - - - - - - - - - 60
MC - - - - - - - - - - - - - - - - - - - 61
MC - - - - - - - - - - - - - - - - - - - 63
MC - - - - - - - - - - - - - - - - - - - 64
MC - - - - - - - - - - - - - - - - - - - 66
MC - - - - - - - - - - - - - - - - - - - 67
MC - - - - - - - - - - - - - - - - - - - 72
MC - - - - - - - - - - - - - - - - - - - 76
MC - - - - - - - - - - - - - - - - - - - 77
MC - - - - - - - - - - - - - - - - - - - 81
RLS - - - - - - - - - - - - - - - - - - - 201
MEP - - - - - - - - - - - - - - - - - - - 165
SWK - - - - - - - - - - - - - - - - - - - 149
EGS - - - - - - - - - - - - - - - - - - - 230

Following a Prophet

JA - - - - - - - - - - - - - - - - - - - 5
ETB - - - - - - - - - - - - - - - - - - - 34
MC - - - - - - - - - - - - - - - - - - - 62
HRJ - - - - - - - - - - - - - - - - - - - 186

Gratitude

ETB - - - - - - - - - - - - - - - - - - - 30
ETB - - - - - - - - - - - - - - - - - - - 34
VLB - - - - - - - - - - - - - - - - - - - 46
MC - - - - - - - - - - - - - - - - - - - 75
PHD - - - - - - - - - - - - - - - - - - - 127
PHD - - - - - - - - - - - - - - - - - - - 130
SWK - - - - - - - - - - - - - - - - - - - 158

Healing of the Sick

MC - - - - - - - - - - - - - - - - - - - 61
MC - - - - - - - - - - - - - - - - - - - 64

MC - - - - - - - - - - - - - - - - - - - 66
MC - - - - - - - - - - - - - - - - - - - 67
MC - - - - - - - - - - - - - - - - - - - 68
MC - - - - - - - - - - - - - - - - - - - 75
MC - - - - - - - - - - - - - - - - - - - 77
MC - - - - - - - - - - - - - - - - - - - 80
MC - - - - - - - - - - - - - - - - - - - 80
MC - - - - - - - - - - - - - - - - - - - 81
MEP - - - - - - - - - - - - - - - - - - - 165
EGS - - - - - - - - - - - - - - - - - - - 226

Humility

MJA - - - - - - - - - - - - - - - - - - - 13
ETB - - - - - - - - - - - - - - - - - - - 27
PHD - - - - - - - - - - - - - - - - - - - 125
SWK - - - - - - - - - - - - - - - - - - - 153
EGS - - - - - - - - - - - - - - - - - - - 234

Inspiration

JA - - - - - - - - - - - - - - - - - - - 7
MC - - - - - - - - - - - - - - - - - - - 78
LCD - - - - - - - - - - - - - - - - - - - 87
LCD - - - - - - - - - - - - - - - - - - - 95
HRJ - - - - - - - - - - - - - - - - - - - 181
SWK - - - - - - - - - - - - - - - - - - - 155
EGS - - - - - - - - - - - - - - - - - - - 236
EGS - - - - - - - - - - - - - - - - - - - 236

Integrity

VLB - - - - - - - - - - - - - - - - - - - 43
PHD - - - - - - - - - - - - - - - - - - - 105
PHD - - - - - - - - - - - - - - - - - - - 129
ARD - - - - - - - - - - - - - - - - - - - 141
HRJ - - - - - - - - - - - - - - - - - - - 190
HRJ - - - - - - - - - - - - - - - - - - - 191
JHV - - - - - - - - - - - - - - - - - - - 192
JHV - - - - - - - - - - - - - - - - - - - 244
JHV - - - - - - - - - - - - - - - - - - - 249
MEP - - - - - - - - - - - - - - - - - - - 175
SWK - - - - - - - - - - - - - - - - - - - 150
SWK - - - - - - - - - - - - - - - - - - - 158

Joy

MJA - - - - - - - - - - - - - - - - - - - 14
ETB - - - - - - - - - - - - - - - - - - - 28
PHD - - - - - - - - - - - - - - - - - - - 119
PHD - - - - - - - - - - - - - - - - - - - 127
RLS - - - - - - - - - - - - - - - - - - - 207
RLS - - - - - - - - - - - - - - - - - - - 210
JHV - - - - - - - - - - - - - - - - - - - 241
MEP - - - - - - - - - - - - - - - - - - - 175

Index

Love

MC	59
MC	70
HRJ	186
RLS	207
RLS	216

Love of Children

MJA	15
MC	60
MC	76
LCD	90
PHD	101
MEP	166
LCD	88

Love of Parents

MC	70
LCD	91
LCD	92
MEP	166

Loyalty

MJA	16
ETB	26
ETB	29
MC	71
RLS	204
JHV	241
MEP	173
SWK	151

Missionary Service

MJA	13
MJA	15
ETB	23
ETB	26
ETB	28
ETB	29
VLB	48
MC	63
PHD	105
PHD	107
ARD	137
RLS	206
JHV	247
JHV	251

Prayer

JA	3
VLB	46

MC	60
MC	64
MC	75
MC	76
HRJ	194
RLS	219
SWK	153
EGS	234

Priesthood

MC	81
MC	81
MC	75
LCD	87
MEP	165
EGS	223
EGS	232
JHV	241

Prophecy

JA	7
SWK	155
EGS	223

Repentance

LCD	93
HRJ	181
MEP	166
EGS	232
JHV	242

Sacrifice

JA	3
PHD	115
ETB	33
ETB	36
MC	70
PHD	122
ARD	141
SWK	151
JHV	250

Testimony

VLB	45
ETB	30
MC	69
MC	77
MC	69
PHD	106
PHD	116

ARD - - - - - - - - - - - - - - - - - - 137
EGS - - - - - - - - - - - - - - - - - - 225
EGS - - - - - - - - - - - - - - - - - - 226
EGS - - - - - - - - - - - - - - - - - - 237

Unity

MC - - - - - - - - - - - - - - - - - - 59
MC - - - - - - - - - - - - - - - - - - 71
LCD - - - - - - - - - - - - - - - - - - 92

EGS - - - - - - - - - - - - - - - - - - 230
EGS - - - - - - - - - - - - - - - - - - 223

Work

ETB - - - - - - - - - - - - - - - - - - 24
MC - - - - - - - - - - - - - - - - - - 63
PHD - - - - - - - - - - - - - - - - - - 101
PHD - - - - - - - - - - - - - - - - - - 115
PHD - - - - - - - - - - - - - - - - - - 120
RLS - - - - - - - - - - - - - - - - - - 202

ALPHABETICAL INDEX

Adopt, 60.

Bear, 88.
Benson, Ezra Taft, 206.
Book of Mormon, 188, 248.
Brazil, 51.
Brown, Hugh B., 211.
Budget, 250.

Camargo, Helio, 51.
Cannons, 213.
Cardinal, 105.
Casper, Billy, 107.
Chickens, 95.
Church College of Hawaii, 47.
Cigarette, 166.
Clark, President J. Reuben, 153, 230.
Coffee, 173.
Communication, 212.
Concentration camp, 130.
Czechoslovakia, 142, 236.

"Dear Abby," 127-8.
Devil, 183.
Dream, 8.
Drugs, 90.
Dunn, Loren C., 186.
Dyer, Alvin R., 186.

East Germany, 141.
Elders quorum, 71.
Excommunicated, 181.

Family home evening, 218.
Football, 129, 210.
Footprints, 175.
Fyans, J. Thomas, 50.

Genealogical records, 139.
Goals, 203.
Grant, Heber J., 3, 7, 27, 155.
Griffith, Andy, 190.

Hardy, Rufus K., 78.
Home teacher, 252.
Home teachers, 247.
House, 123.
Hugo, Victor, 202.
Humility, 234.

Interest, 243.

Jitney, 242.

Kennedy, David, 206.
Killebrew, Harmon, 116.
Knight, Jesse, 3.

Lee, Harold B., 181.
Lincoln, Abe, 190.
Lineage, 236.
Lombardi, Vince, 129.

Marine, 45.
Marriott, Willard, 207.
McKay, David O., 5, 27, 119, 186.
McKay, Thomas E., 165.
Mexico, 50.
Microfilming, 139.
Missionary, returned, 25; Mormon, 26.

Page, Satchel, 249.
Piano, 115.
Poland, 139.
Polio, 62, 64.
Pop, 192.
Pratt, Orson, 8.
Priesthood order, 233.
Prophet, the, 183.

Refugees, 33.
Relief Society, secretary of, 64.
Reverend Givens, 217.
Romney, George, 206.
Rowberry, Patriarch, 7.
Rules, 210.

Sacrament, 73.
Sailor, 48, 73.
Seiler, Arnold, 141.
Sill, Sterling W., 192.
Silver dollar, 16.
Smith, George Albert, 31, 63.
"Smith, Joseph," 113.
Smith, Joseph, 228.
Smoot, Reed, 3.
Snow, Eliza R., 7
Sorority, 110.
Sound, 213.
South Vietnam, 46.
Stroke, 195.
Tabernacle Choir, 36.
Taxicab, 66.

Testimony, 225.
Three Nephites, 109.
Tithing, 158.
Tongan, 46.
Toronto, Wallace, 236.
Translation, 49.
Typhoid, 68.

Uelzen, 230.
Unity, 230.

Uranium, 228.

Warsaw, 140.
Waterfall, 207.
Whaanga, Albert, 78.
Wilson, Joseph Smith, 188.
Wool, 244.

"Young, Brigham," 113.
Young, Zina D., 7.